But Do You Feel Safe with Him?

10 Reasons
Why Performing Femininity
Never Works in Love

Umm Zakiyyah

But Do You Feel Safe with Him?
10 Reasons Why Performing Femininity Never Works in Love
by Umm Zakiyyah

ISBN: 978-1-942985-20-4
Library of Congress Control Number: 2025903101

- Join Feminine Soul Reset (FSR) at **SQsoul.com**
- UZ Books at **uzauthor.com** or bulk orders at wholesale@ummzakiyyah.com
- UZ Courses at **uzhearthub.com** and **uzuniversity.com**

Arabic script of Qur'an from legacy.quran.com

Translation of meanings of verses from Qur'an adapted from Saheeh International, Darussalam, and Yusuf Ali translations.

Published by Al-Walaa Publications
Dallas, Texas (USA)

TABLE OF CONTENTS

Section/Part/Chapter	Page
Author's Note: *Why This Book*	8
Dear Reader: *How to Read This Book*	10
INTRODUCTION	15
Overcoming Roadblocks to Embodying Femininity	
i. Two Sides of Performing Femininity	16
ii. Performing Femininity Can Shift within a Relationship	18
iii. The Essence of Masculinity and Femininity	21
iv. The Essence of Something vs. the Essence of Someone	23
v. The Ten Sections and Why Performing Femininity Is So Harmful	29
PART ONE	31
What Is Performing Femininity?	
1. He Wanted a Feminine Wife and Daughters	32
2. What Does Femininity Mean to You?	35
3. What Does It Mean to Be Feminine, Truly?	38
4. Why Most Women Perform Femininity	40
5. How Muslims Islamicize Women's Self-Abandonment	44
6. In Islam, a Woman's Life, Body, and Soul Are Her Own	47
7. Seeking Male Approval Can Become Self-Destructive and Addictive	49
8. Why Performing Femininity Is So Emotionally Addictive	53
9. The Making of a "Good Woman"	56
PART TWO	58
TEN REASONS	
Why Performing Femininity Never Works in Love	
Reason One: True Love Requires Authenticity	59
10. A Good Girl Learning to Be Good	60
11. Who's the Boss?	63
12. The Overachiever of Survival Mode	65
Reason Two: Love Is About Being Fully Seen, Performing Is About Hiding	70
13. Perfecting the Art of Being Invisible	71

14. Getting to Know My New Bosses 73

15. Enduring It All for the Sake of Allah 75

16. The Sin of Being Seen or Heard 77

17. We See with Our Hearts, Not Our Eyes 79

18. Harming Others for the Sake of Allah 82

Reason Three: Performing Asks Women to Show Up Empty, Love Asks Women to Show Up Full 87

19. The Boy at the Skating Rink 88

20. An Empty Vessel and Blank Slate? 92

21. Pretty Packaging at the Lowest Cost 95

22. Women's Fairytales and Unrealistic Expectations? 98

Reason Four: Healthy Love Nurtures Living a Full Life, Performing for Love Extinguishes It 102

23. The High Value Woman of Non-Existence 103

24. What Exactly Did "Good Girls" Have to Begin With? 105

25. The Highly Valued Submissive Providers 107

26. Wow Him with Your Talents, Then Throw It All Away 110

27. If I Make Myself Small, Will You Love Me "Big"? 112

28. The Step-by-Step Revival of Burying Females Alive 114

29. Understanding Benevolent Misogyny 118

Reason Five: True Love Always Starts Within, Performing Femininity Requires an External Script 123

30. What Men Like 124

31. Is It Really All That Important, Though? 127

32. Men Want to Feel Safe with You Too 129

The Feminine Warrior 133

33. What Does a Feminine Woman Look Like, Truly? 134

Reason Six: You Can't Perform Femininity and Embody Femininity At Once 139

When Women Are Asked to Lead Their Men 140

34. True Femininity Is Rooted in Authenticity 141

35. True Femininity Is Varied and Complex 143

Are You Performing Femininity or Embodying Femininity? 146

36. Auditioning for Love Extinguishes Joy and Authenticity 147

37. Performing Femininity vs. Embodying Femininity 149

38. The Wounded Feminine Performs for the   151
    Wounded Masculine

Reason Seven: If You Don't Love You, He Can't
Love You   156

39. I Knew I Was Ugly   157
40. She Thought She Was Fat   160
    Performance, a Dictionary Definition   165
41. Why We Perform for Love   166
42. A Bottomless Vessel Cannot Hold Love   168

When You Embody Femininity, You Live in Holistic
    Spiritual Femininity   170

43. What Does Embodying Femininity Look Like?   171

Reason Eight: Love Is About Connection,
Performing Is About Entertainment   176

44. Clarifying Performing Femininity   177
45. Living Outside-In vs. Inside-Out   179
46. Being vs. Doing   181

Performative Roles Require Emotional Dysregulation   183

47. Rational Men and Emotional Women: The Dance   184
    of Masculine and Feminine Dysregulation

Performative Roles Lead to Body-Mind Disconnect,
    Emotional Dysregulation and Disconnection   189

When Men Close Their Hearts, the World Suffers   190

48. Avoiding Emotional Dysregulation Is the Sunnah   191
49. Independent Women Are Often the Most   195
    Compassionate, Feminine, Emotionally Regulated
    Wives
    Are Alpha Males Natural Leaders?   198
50. Performative Manhood Fixates on the Alpha Male   199
    Of Monikers and Men   201
51. Was the Prophet صلى a Beta Male?   202

Healthier Connection Means Healthier Boundaries   210

52. Seven Signs You're Performing for Love   211

But Shouldn't We Want to Please Our Husbands?   214

Reason Nine: Love Requires Trust, Performance   218
Implies Distrust

53. True Love Requires Trust and Emotional Safety   219
54. Performing Femininity Is About Distrusting   221
    Yourself and Men
    Toxic Stability   224

55. Trust Men's Inner Experience, But Not Women's?   225
56. Prioritizing a Woman's Joy, Comfort, and   228
Wellness Can Save a Relationship
57. Performing Femininity Fuels Hypervigilance and   230
Centers Unrighteous Men

Reason Ten: Love and Unsafety Cannot Coexist   234
58. They Need to Constantly Feel Superior, Not Safe   235
to You
59. We Need to Stay Small and Unthreatening, Not   237
Safe or Protected

Power Plays, Victimhood, and Entitlement   239
60. We Become Experts at Self-Protection Because   240
Our Men Don't See Us
61. We Learn to Smile When We Want to Cry and   242
Agree When We Want to Say
62. He Only Wants Good Food, Good Sex, and Quiet   244
Submission

But Do You Feel Emotionally Safe with Him?   246
63. The Dangers of Submission Before Safety   247
64. Being a "Good Woman" Almost Killed Her   249
65. Men Set the Temperature of a Relationship,   252
Women Nurture It

It Feels Good to Let Him Lead   255
66. Feelings of Safety Inspire Surrender and   256
Submission
67. Performing Femininity Disconnects You from   258
Female Pleasure

RE-CAP: Review of Essentials and   260
Compassionate Accountability Prompts
68. Surrender to Uncomfortable Self-Honesty and   264
Compassionate Accountability
69. But Why Am I Choosing Unsafety?   268
PART THREE   271
Let's Heal Together and Love Together:
Five Ways Forward
70. Who Will Catch Her When She Falls?   272
71. Who Will Step Up First?   274
FIVE STEPS   276
Toward Mutual Love and Intimacy
72. Take Responsibility for Your Own Life and Soul   277

73. Prioritize Your Relationship with Your Creator   279
and Yourself

74. Get Curious Alone and Together   281

75. Give Each Other Space to Enjoy Life   282

76. Forgive and Overlook As a Lifestyle   283

Epilogue: Believe in Unseen Possibilities of Love and   284
Intimacy

Read an excerpt from: *Before You Become His Garment in*   286
Marriage: Do's and Don'ts for Muslim Women

Glossary of Select Arabic and Islamic Terms   293

References   295

About the Author   298

Read FREE Books by Umm Zakiyyah   300

Author's Note
Why This Book

This collection began as part of the book and course series entitled, *He's Scared to Love You, You're Scared to Love Yourself*, currently scheduled as part of Feminine Soul Reset at sqsoul.com. However, due to the layered complexity of the topic of "performing femininity"—which is arguably the most common form of emotional self-abandonment and fear of self-love in women—I decided to extract from my manuscript and course-notes those parts that relate to this aspect of the wounded feminine.

Because of my desire to make this current discussion as simple, straightforward, and beneficial as possible, I intentionally keep the chapter sections relatively short. As such, the reader might find that she (or he) has deeper questions or reflections about a topic after completing a particular section or even after completing the book itself. This is intentional.

For this particular topic, it is not my goal to offer definitive answers or conclusions about the phenomenon of performing femininity in women. Instead, the goal of this publication is to inspire within the reader inner examination, self-awareness, and compassionate accountability. As you self-reflect on what this discussion brings up for you, you might find that many of the answers and conclusions you seek are already deep inside of you—or at least within your reach through resources such as therapy, support groups, or loving relationships around you.

Even still, I pray that this book's brief glimpse into the topic of performing femininity proves more inspirational, informative, and beneficial than you could have ever imagined or hoped for when you first began reading.

Sincerely,
Your sister in faith and hope,

Umm Zakiyyah
January 17, 2025
17th of Rajab 1446AH

Dear Reader
How to Read This Book

"To learn life-changing material is much more than an intellectual exercise; it involves your mind, body, emotions, and ultimately your spirit...This material is the work of a lifetime. Give yourself plenty of permission to learn, make mistakes, correct, and relearn. In short, be easy with yourself as you work with these new ideas."
—Gay and Kathlyn Hendricks, PhDs, *Conscious Loving: The Journey to Co-Commitment*

As you begin this book, feel free to read the parts, sections, and chapters in any order that feels most authentic, most beneficial, or most enjoyable for you. For some readers, this will mean reading chronologically, beginning with the Introduction and Part One and then going on to Part Two and then Part Three. For other readers, this will mean reading Part Two (or Three) first and then going back to Part One and the Introduction. For still other readers, this will mean browsing the Table of Contents and then reading only the chapters, sections, or parts that appeal to them specifically.

Nevertheless, for the greatest benefit and understanding of what is being discussed, I strongly encourage readers to read the book in full, even if the parts and chapters of the book are not read in chronological order. At the same time, I do believe reading the book in the order that is presented allows for the greatest understanding and benefit of the topics discussed.

Additionally, I encourage readers to read and respond to (or at least sincerely reflect on) the prompts at the end of each section in the second part of this book which details the ten reasons why performing femininity never works in love. These interactive prompts are entitled "RE-CAP" (Review of Essentials and Compassionate Accountability Prompts), as explained below.

RE-CAP:
Review of Essentials *and*
Compassionate Accountability Prompts

In Part Two in particular, I break down the ten reasons why performing femininity never works in love. In this second part of the book, you'll notice that each section/reason ends with what I call a RE-CAP. This is an acronym that stands for Review of Essentials and Compassionate Accountability Prompts. These recaps of the essential points of each section, along with journal prompts and activities, are designed to provide the female reader with foundational tools for shifting away from performing femininity and beginning her journey toward embodying femininity. These prompts and activities should be done in a space of self-compassion while also holding yourself accountable for the self-awareness, personal honesty, and self-correction necessary to transition from performative womanhood to embodied womanhood. However, for the purposes of this book, we'll be focusing most on self-awareness, as this is the foundation of all healing and transformation.

Naturally, completing these RE-CAP compassionate accountability prompts are not required or necessary, and you can certainly benefit from this book without them. At the same time, I do encourage the female reader (and even the male reader, wherever relevant) to at least mentally engage with these prompts. Also, I encourage the reader to skip any prompt that she (or he) finds too upsetting, overwhelming, or triggering.

Most importantly, after responding to any prompt (even if only mentally) that brings up sadness, agitation, or emotional overwhelm; I strongly encourage you to implement some simple steps (e.g., slow deep breaths and exhales, box-breathing, meditation, etc.) to bring your mind, body, and nervous system back to a state of *anaah* (inner calm).

I also encourage every reader to additionally seek the assistance of a trauma-informed mental health professional, especially for any persistent distressing thoughts, feelings, or overwhelming emotions that come to the surface as you read this book and/or participate in the RE-CAP prompts and activities. While I'm confident that this book can be beneficial to any reader committed to self-honesty and self-betterment, it is important to remember that it cannot take the place of professional therapy.

Also, as you read and reflect, remember to take care of yourself and take your time. There's no rush. And remember, there's no better version of you that needs to exist right now. **The only thing you need at this very moment is to compassionately accept yourself for who you are and where you are on your journey**, even if it's not where you want to be. Then go from there.

Or just sit still without trying to go anywhere right now—except insomuch as you do the bare minimum that your soul needs to connect to your Merciful Rabb each day. Then read this book from that space of compassionate presence and inner acceptance. In other words, as I like to remind myself when I'm feeling overwhelmed, anxious, or overly self-critical: *Just be and let it be.*

To the Non-Muslim Reader

Naturally, because I am a Muslim woman navigating the reality of this topic in my faith community, significant portions of this book will be shared through the lens of Islamic spirituality. However, due to the universality of the topic of performative womanhood, even outside the context of religion, I'm confident that readers of all backgrounds, even those without a faith tradition, can benefit from this discussion.

For most relatively unfamiliar religious terminology or commonly used Arabic words, I've provided a Glossary at the end of this book. Also, whenever you come upon a word you don't understand, feel free to do a quick internet search for its definition, especially if the context doesn't make the meaning clear.

To the Grammar Police

In certain sentences and sections in this book, you'll notice that I deviate from what is technically correct from a grammatical point of view. I do this to lean more into what I call "the language of the heart." So, no, my occasional switching of tenses, mismatched pronoun-antecedent usage, sentence fragments, and use of certain verbs as nouns (e.g., overwhelm) isn't an oversight. It's aimed at inspiring the reader to open their heart to the enigmatic world of love and their own human *nafs* (inner world). So, relax your mind, put down your proverbial "red pen" and allow your heart to humbly receive whatever benefit your Merciful Creator has already written for you.

For the female soul seeking to love herself in all her beautiful imperfection. May you forever embrace your quirky uniqueness for the divine gift it is.

INTRODUCTION
Overcoming Roadblocks to Embodying Femininity

"Make every effort to change things you do not like. If you cannot make a change, change the way you have been thinking. You might find a new solution."
—Maya Angelou, *Letter to My Daughter*

Two Sides of Performing Femininity

Because this topic is admittedly complex, I dedicate Part One of this book to discussing the question "What Is Performing Femininity?" During this initial discussion, I mention some brief points from the mental health perspective while also briefly touching on the Islamic point of view regarding woman's full personhood. However, in this part, as in the rest of the book, I intentionally avoid delving too deeply into mental health research or Islamic evidences surrounding certain points. This is to preserve the relatively lighthearted tone of this book and to make the book more accessible to a wider audience, as extensive scholarly discussions, whether secular or religious, tend to become cumbersome to the average reader.

In Part Two, I divide the discussion into ten sections, corresponding to the ten reasons that performing femininity never works in love. The ten sections in Part Two focus on two sides of performing femininity: (1) how it is cultivated by emotional trauma, personal experience, and cultural programming and (2) how it is inherently contradictory, problematic, and self-destructive by nature.

In Part Two, I begin the first side of this discussion by sharing how my own life experiences, as well as those of other women, shape our earliest ideas about ourselves, about the world around us, and about how we should show up for the men in our lives (or for the men we *hope* to be in our lives). Amidst these reflections, I share very specific reasons why performing femininity doesn't have the ability to work in a healthy relationship rooted in true love, which by definition is mutually nourishing to both the man and the woman.

Finally, in Part Three I discuss five steps that both men and women can implement individually, as a couple, and as a community to cultivate mutual love and intimacy amongst us. I also briefly discuss the importance of men, wherever possible, taking the lead in this collective healing between men and women, and I also discuss why I make this suggestion.

In the next few sections of this introduction, I discuss the foundations of shifting from performing femininity to embodying femininity. I also briefly discuss the importance of understanding why the essence of masculinity is not limited to the male experience and the essence of femininity is not limited to the female experience, although in this book I dedicate most of the discussion of performing femininity (and masculinity) to the male-female dichotomy.

Performing Femininity Can Shift within a Relationship

Given the sensitive nature of this book topic as it relates to the personal lives of many readers, it is important to note, in fact *emphasize* the following point: Performing femininity certainly *can* be transformed into true femininity within a relationship itself. In other words, it is not necessary for a woman to leave her current relationship, cancel any wedding plans, or dissolve her marriage when consciously shifting from performing femininity to embodying true femininity.

This is the case even if a woman finds herself feeling "trapped" in cycles of performing femininity in her current circumstance. In the context of marriage, the woman's personal transformation becomes possible when two variables are present: (1) the woman is in a safe relationship and environment and (2) the woman is fully willing and committed to doing her own inner work. (For Muslim women interested in investing in this personal transformation, I encourage them to seek the guidance of professional therapy along with joining our Feminine Soul Reset membership at sqsoul.com where they are guided step-by-step through this process).

With regards to number 1, by "safe relationship" I mean the woman is not being actively harmed or abused by her husband, whether physically, verbally, or spiritually. I do <u>not</u> mean the woman must be in an environment of deeply felt emotional safety, as this emotionally attuned relational state occurs only after both the man and woman heal their underlying emotional wounding (which was inciting them to perform masculinity and femininity in the relationship).

Ideally, the woman shifting from performing femininity to embodying spiritual femininity (i.e., *taqwaa*-centered womanhood) will also have a supportive, emotionally secure man by her side who is also doing his own inner work. However, at the very least, her husband should not be *resistant* to this positive, soul-nourishing upgrade in her life and their relationship. And by resistant, I mean he is unsafe and/or *consistently* oppositional to her efforts toward emotional self-investment (with the operative words being both "unsafe" and "consistently oppositional"). I do <u>not</u> mean he is occasionally resistant to her changes in moments of friction, triggers, or disagreements, as <u>all</u> efforts toward positive transformation will hit roadblocks and resistance, not only in the relationship itself but also within the person herself (or himself).

Nevertheless, it is important to note, in fact emphasize, that a woman successfully shifting from performing femininity to embodying femininity almost *never* requires the enthusiastic approval, support, or participation of another person, not even her own husband. If a woman feels that she does in fact require this level of support, again (as aforementioned), I encourage a combination of professional therapy along with the compassionate accountability community of women at Feminine Soul Reset. When a woman seeks her most intensive support outside the context of her relationship, she often finds that her husband himself becomes fully supportive of her efforts. Additionally, while witnessing the positive changes in his wife's private life and relationship with him and the children, it is not uncommon for a man to become genuinely curious as to how he himself can benefit from a similar upgrade in his life, mindset, and relationship with his soul.

As I hope will become clear by the end of the book, the reason that it is unnecessary (and often unwise) for a woman to make a life-altering decision such as dissolving an entire relationship in an effort to eliminate performing femininity from her life is quite simple: More than anything, shifting from performing femininity to embodying true femininity is an *individual* emotional and spiritual journey rather than a joint relationship journey. Therefore, this transformation almost never requires that you take this personal journey along with another person (unless, of course, you are in need of professional therapy or a support group designated for this purpose).

Nevertheless, it is absolutely true that this individual journey is certainly *enhanced* when you are blessed with a man who is also consciously shifting from performing masculinity to embodying spiritual masculinity (i.e., he is becoming more intentional about implementing *taqwaa*-centered manhood at home and in community). Fortunately, however, many sincere men are inspired to make this conscious shift after witnessing the woman they love make positive changes in her own life.

iii

The Essence of Masculinity and Femininity

Before beginning this book's discussion on performing femininity, it is important to highlight this point: It is in the practical manifestations of wounded masculinity and wounded femininity that we begin to witness the immense complexity and multiple nuances of this topic. These nuances and complexities go far beyond the male experience with himself and the world around him and far beyond the confines of the female experience with herself and the world around her.

In a nutshell, we can think of both masculine wounding and feminine wounding as causing harm in how they manifest in the world. Both masculine and feminine wounding stem from unhealed emotional wounds that incite us to consciously or unconsciously fixate on external ideas of what it means to be a "real man" or a "good woman." This external fixation often comes at the expense of our own wellness and inner contentment and ultimately disconnects us from—and shames us away from—showing up as our full authentic selves.

However, masculine wounding causes the most obvious harm to realities and experiences outside the self, and feminine wounding causes the most obvious harm to realities and experiences within the self. This is why, for example, a man's wounding can often be seen in how poorly he treats his loved ones, and a woman's wounding can often be seen in how poorly she treats herself. In their extreme forms, masculine wounding manifests as verbal or physical abuse of others, and feminine wounding manifests as severe depression, stress-induced illness, toxic victimhood, or any other mental or physiological state that makes it extremely difficult or impossible to healthily complete daily tasks and responsibilities. Nevertheless, both types of wounding cause harm to the self *and* others (e.g., masculine wounding is rooted in a toxic relationship with oneself, and feminine wounding leads to neglecting one's children and/or to the parentification of them).

Though a detailed discussion of masculine and feminine wounding is beyond the scope of this book, it is crucial to understand this point: Manifestations of wounded masculinity are not confined to men, and manifestations of wounded femininity are not confined to women (e.g., a man can be severely depressed to the point of immobility, and a woman can be verbally or physically abusive of others). This is mainly because in both the human experience and in the nature of the world itself, the essence of *something* is different from the essence of *someone*. Evidence of this universal law, which applies to everything in existence (seen and unseen), is inherent in the classical Arabic language that Allah has chosen for His final revelation to humankind, as discussed briefly in the next section.

The Essence of Something vs. the Essence of Someone

In the Qur'an itself we see how the essence of *something* like the human *nafs*, which is the human's inner world, is grammatically feminine. However, we also see how the essence of *someone* whose body holds this *nafs*, is either grammatically masculine (in the case of a male) or grammatically feminine (in the case of a female). Similarly, every noun and verb in the Arabic language has an essence that is either masculine or feminine depending on the practical way that this thing or person shows up in its world, whether that world is apparent or hidden (or seen or unseen).

As it relates to Arabic nouns in particular, there are no exceptions to this. Even the word *Allah* in Arabic is grammatically masculine. However, Allah Himself is neither male nor female, because being male or female is a characteristic of creation, and the Creator is nothing like His creation.

How is all of this relevant to the discussion of performing femininity? Well, let's mention five (5) points that are either directly or indirectly related to the various discussions of emotional wounding on the male and female *nafs* that are explored later in this book:

1) The wounded masculine needs to *feel* that he is providing safety and protection to the female soul (even though he is, in fact, not providing it). In fact,

the wounded masculine's entire identity as a man is rooted in *feelings* of manhood as opposed to actual manhood as defined and assigned by God.

2) Due to point number 1, the wounded feminine is absolutely essential to the unhealed man's identity and sense of self. This is because it is only the wounded feminine—the woman who is performing femininity instead of authentically embodying it—who is *more* invested in making a man *feel like* a "real man" than in actually benefiting from a real man of *taqwaa* in truth.

3) Both the wounded feminine and the wounded masculine perform for the male gaze. This performative behavior isn't about the essence of who these women and men really are deep inside; rather it is about the essence of their very real wounds (and all of us, without exception, will have very real emotional wounds that need our compassion and healing at some point in our lives).

For the unhealed man in particular, his emotional wounding incites him to use the collective male gaze (and subsequent male approval of his "good performance" of masculine behaviors) as a standard for his own manhood while simultaneously (and sometimes desperately) also seeking admiration and desirability from women. For this reason, a woman who does not center men or the collective male gaze and instead chooses to live in embodied femininity (e.g., an "independent woman" who is emotionally healthy and secure in the life that she is living) is a threat to this man's very identity and sense of manhood (which is rooted in his wounding instead of the essence of his *fitrah*)—just as she is a threat to the unhealed woman's very identity and sense of womanhood (which is rooted in her wounding instead of the essence of her *fitrah*).

As a result, a healthily independent woman living in true femininity and personal authenticity, for example, becomes the scapegoat for all the low self-worth that lives inside the unhealed *nafs* of the wounded masculine and wounded feminine alike. Thus, they project onto this emotionally healthy woman their own inner feelings of low worth and inauthenticity, claiming that she is not a "good woman" or that she is "un-feminine."

4) As mentioned in the previous section, manifestations of wounded masculinity are not confined to men, and manifestations of wounded femininity are not confined to women. Therefore, a woman can externalize her emotional pain by treating her loved ones in obviously harmful and abusive ways (while simultaneously claiming her behavior is inspired by love and protection). Similarly, a man can internalize his emotional pain by "closing in on himself" and becoming immobilized by depression and anxiety until he, for example, becomes neglectful of his loved ones (while simultaneously telling himself and others a story of victimhood that absolves him from showing up fully and responsibly to his own life).

5) This (i.e., point number 4) is mainly because in both the human experience and in the nature of the world itself, the essence of *something* is different from the essence of *someone*.

You Are Not Your Challenges

Here it is relevant to note that the above five points are <u>not</u> about blaming or shaming anyone for their very real personal challenges or mental health issues. The truth of the matter is that every single one of us—without exception—has personal challenges in our lives and varying levels of unwellness that negatively affect our mental and physical health, and even our spiritual practice. In this, some of us are struggling with much deeper challenges than others.

Moreover, some of us have even been diagnosed with very specific physical illnesses or mental health issues, many of which began as unhealed emotional wounds stemming from childhood. In any case, no matter our individual struggle, challenge, or diagnosis (known or unknown), it is important to remember this point: *You are not your struggle, you are not your challenge, and you are not your diagnosis.* In other words, you are not your wounds.

The essence of your challenge is not equal to the essence of you. As such, not a single one of your underlying struggles, challenges, or diagnoses is your fault. Your accountability—like the accountability of every daughter (or son) of Adam in this world—rests in how you *respond* to these struggles, challenges, or diagnoses. Thus, the essence of you is reflected in how sincerely and consistently you show up for yourself (and others) amidst these divinely decreed worldly trials. The essence of you is not reflected in the intricacies or darknesses of the trial itself.

And please remember these two (2) points as you embark on this path of self-healing and personal transformation:

1) Your journey is less about perfection than it is about commitment.
2) Your success is less about "winning" than it is about never giving up.

Thus, your success lies in your perseverance in nurturing the beautiful essence of you, not in any external measurement of success—or with any "happily ever after" relationship with someone else.

Understanding Performative Roles in Men and Women

In the context of this book, it is important to understand the essence of "performing" as distinct from striving for good.

In this discussion, I use the terms *performing* and *performative* to mean that the woman (or man) is showing up to life similar to how an actress (or actor) shows up to a theatre production. So, the woman's (or man's) life becomes effectively about putting on a performance similar to how a stage performer's job is to put on a good show. Here, the only difference is that in performing femininity (and masculinity), the "theatre stage" is the person's own life.

Consequently, the woman shows up in a performative role of womanhood and the man shows up in a performative role of manhood with the sole (or primary) intention of getting a good "performance review" based on some external manmade checklist of femininity and masculinity. As a result, fulfilling the authentic role of being one's true self as an individual woman or man isn't only *not* in the job description; it further contradicts it. Thus, the job of "femininity" and "masculinity" is something entirely different from personal authenticity.

Nonetheless, it is important to note that from a semantic point of view, there is a healthy, positive meaning of the term *job performance* as it relates to womanhood and manhood in this world. For example, when we are sincerely studying what it means to be a "good woman" or "good man" in truth—e.g., by reading the Qur'an, learning about the prophetic example, and reflecting on the lives of righteous women and men of the past—we are using these descriptions and lessons as external guideposts and sources of inspiration for our own journeys of womanhood and manhood in this world. As a result, we naturally aspire to "perform" our own roles of wife and mother (or husband and father) well.

This specific meaning of successfully performing a particular feminine or masculine role in life is not only praiseworthy but also necessary and reflects taking personal responsibility for our lives and how we show up as spouses and parents. As a matter of fact, every sincere human being who is striving for goodness and self-betterment in this world *needs* external examples to help them along the way. These external examples serve as guidance to help us see how well we are "measuring up" to what or whom we aspire to be.

Nevertheless, this particular definition of a good "job performance" is not what is being discussed through the term *performing femininity (or masculinity)* in this book—except insomuch as our intentional, sincere embodiment of true femininity and true masculinity manifests in healthy, soul-nourishing ways that align with the external guideposts given to us by our Creator and His Messenger (peace be upon him). In that case, we would not be discussing performing femininity or masculinity; we would be discussing embodying it.

The Ten Sections and Why Performing Femininity Is So Harmful

The ten sections of this book deal with both sides of performing femininity (i.e., women's real-life experiences and why performing femininity simply *cannot* work in any healthy, loving relationship). As such, this book comprises the following ten reasons why performing femininity never works in love:

(1) True love requires authenticity (i.e., showing up as your true self) while performing femininity, by definition, requires showing up while performing an "act" that has been scripted for you.

(2) Love is about being fully seen (and heard) while performing femininity is about hiding and suppressing your voice.

(3) Performing femininity asks women to show up empty while true love asks women to show up full.

(4) Healthy love supports living a full, joyful life while performing-for-love stunts inner fulfillment and extinguishes joy.

(5) True love always starts within, yet performing femininity requires an external, manmade script.

(6) You cannot perform femininity and embody femininity at the same time.

(7) If you don't love you, he can't love you.

(8) Love is about connection while performing is about entertainment.

(9) Love requires trust while performance implies distrust.

(10) Love and unsafety cannot coexist in a healthy, loving relationship (and performing femininity is often rooted in women feeling emotionally unsafe to show up as their true selves).

Perhaps the most serious harm of performing femininity is found in reason number 10, because it keeps women locked in a space of feeling unsafe—within herself and within her relationship. Moreover, when this lack of safety is precisely what a man wants (or demands) from a woman— as is the case with men living in an extreme form of the wounded masculine—then equating performing femininity with praiseworthy things like piety, female goodness, and being a righteous wife can cost a woman her life, literally.

Whether this loss of life is due to the "slow death" incited by the steady shutdown of her nervous system over time, or due to sudden external physical harm inflicted by her husband; almost nothing good comes from a woman living in perpetual harm (emotionally or physically) while imagining she's just being a good, "feminine" woman. When a woman lives in this constant state of emotional and/or physical unsafety to gain the approval or pleasure of the man she loves, her experience gets to the very heart of the central question of this book: *But do you feel safe with him?*

PART ONE
What Is Performing Femininity?

"So often as women, we spend so much of our lives auditioning and performing for a man's heart, wondering if he'll be the one to finally choose us. It is only after years of this exhaustive tap dancing that we come to realize we should have focused on winning our own hearts and choosing our own selves."
—from the journal of Umm Zakiyyah

1

He Wanted a Feminine Wife and Daughters

"I just feel so blessed to be here," she said, averting her eyes nervously.

Quietly, we listened. We were a group of about twenty women, mostly non-Arab, and it was our first day at a small neighborhood Qur'an school in Riyadh, Saudi Arabia. At the time, I was living as an American expat there teaching English in the mornings and early afternoons and then studying Qur'an and Arabic in the late afternoons and evenings.

"I wasn't allowed to study Qur'an before I came here," she said, her voice shaking a bit. "None of us were."

"What do you mean?" we asked. "None of who?"

"The girls," she said. "The women," she added. "My father didn't allow it." She explained that along with herself, neither her mother nor any of her sisters or female relatives were allowed to read, study, or memorize the Qur'an.

The room grew silent momentarily.

"But why?" I asked, unable to contain myself.

"My father said girls don't need an education because they don't need it for marriage," she explained. "So, growing up, we were only allowed to learn things like cooking and cleaning, and we were forbidden to learn to read, or study books or anything like that."

"Not even the Qur'an?" I said, shocked.

She shook her head sadly. "No, but it's like that in our whole village. None of the girls are allowed."

Wow. I didn't even know what to say to that.

"But *alhamdulillaah*, my husband lets me study Qur'an."

The words "lets me" incited in me a complicated mixture of emotions that I wouldn't be able to name for many years, but at that moment, I stayed silent, listening intently and disturbed greatly.

"That's why I feel so blessed to be here," she continued. "I'm thankful to my husband for taking us out of our country and moving us here." Some of us asked what country she and her husband had moved from, and she said Afghanistan.

"But if your husband supports you, why did you have to leave your country to study Qur'an?" I asked.

"He could get into a lot of trouble with my father and the other men there," she explained. "So, we decided it's best for him to just pretend like he agrees with them until we could leave and come here." A hint of a smile formed on her face. "And now, I can finally learn to read," she said, joyful gratitude in those words.

The bittersweet sadness that settled over the room that day—and in my heart—is something I don't think I'll ever forget.

Not Exactly a Rare Exception

At the time that I'm writing this, it has been over fifteen years since I sat in that circle of women in Riyadh, Saudi Arabia. Yet it wasn't until one early morning about five years ago after I had long since returned home to the United States of America that I actually cried about it for the first time.

I was sitting in the prayer room of my Maryland townhome that day and reciting aloud from the very *mus'haf* (all-Arabic Qur'an) that I'd held in my hands the day that I listened to the Afghani woman share her story. It was then that it all came back to me suddenly.

The tears flowed from a deep place inside me. It was a carefully hidden place in my *nafs* that had sheltered my own spiritual heartbreak and emotional wounding for years. And it was only in that moment that I could cry because before then, I wasn't broken or brave enough to even acknowledge that it was there.

I cried because I felt in that moment the heavy grief I had been carrying, which was a weighty mixture of my own grief and the Afghani woman's, as well as the grief of so many Muslim girls and women who didn't even know they had lost something worth grieving—or that they needed someone to cry for them.

I cried, too, because not enough girls or women understood until it was too late that the story of the Afghani woman (and of her husband who'd be severely punished and socially ostracized for supporting her) is not a rare exception, though we'd like so very much for it to be. No, *we* likely will never be forbidden from learning to read or write or to memorize the Qur'an. Nevertheless, every day we internalize harmful messages about ourselves and what it means to be a "good woman."

Then on this path of internalizing harm—which we imagine will secure for us lasting love—we work so hard to erase ourselves, to stuff down our desires and feelings, to muffle our voices and our dreams, and to even sacrifice parts of our very own souls, thus giving up our spiritual wellness. All of this we do in hopes of becoming more "feminine" and less ourselves.

2

What Does Femininity Mean to You?

If you prefer, feel free to merely read through this exercise while reflecting on your responses mentally. Then come back to it later to write down your answers in a personal journal. Just be sure to make a mental note of your initial thoughts. Alternatively, record your reflections via speaking into a voice memo app or audio recording device.

Self-Reflection

Look deep within and be honest with yourself as you ask yourself the questions below. Then using a private journal or a separate piece of paper, write freely from your heart based on the *first* responses that come to mind with each question. Be as brief or as detailed as you like.

This means writing freely without overthinking and without trying to give the "right" response. There are no right or wrong answers here. The goal of this exercise is to understand yourself, your mindset, and your own feelings around femininity. Remember, the only audience for this exercise is your own soul, as no one else will see it (unless you show it to them):

(1) What are the first three words that come to mind when you think of a "feminine woman"? What traits come to mind when you think of a woman "living in her femininity"?

(2) Why do you think these specific words or traits come to mind? What makes these words and traits feel

"feminine" to you? How are they evidence of a woman "living in her femininity"?

(3) How would *you* define "femininity" or being feminine specifically? Why did you choose this particular meaning of the term?

(4) Where did you first learn these concepts (in your description and definition) of femininity and of being feminine? In your view, does your definition of femininity or being feminine align with what you genuinely believe your Creator wants for *every* female soul in this world? Why or why not?

(5) Do you believe there are parts of femininity that you yourself have not yet properly understood or embodied in your life? If yes, how so? Where do think your limitations come from? If you answered no, where do you think your proper understanding and embodiment of femininity come from?

Are We Oversimplifying Femininity?

In responding to the journal prompts about what femininity and being feminine mean to you, chances are, if you're like most of us (myself included), the first words that came to mind align with traits like *soft-spoken*, *timid*, and *submissive*.

However, as we shall see later in this book, while these traits can certainly align with *some* manifestations of femininity in women, they do not encompass femininity as a whole. More importantly, they do not give a balanced, holistic, complex picture of what it means to be a pious woman as defined by our Merciful Creator.

In His infinite wisdom, our Merciful Rabb created and perfectly designed the intricate manifestation of the female soul in this world. In this, He gifted her with a uniquely assigned mind, body, and spirit, all of which embody and amplify her unique personality in this world.

3

What Does It Mean to Be Feminine, Truly?

Throughout the remainder of this book, I challenge each of us (myself included) to turn the lens inward and examine our own hidden wounds. Through this inner examination, I hope to inspire each of us—most especially myself—to carefully and humbly acknowledge how we show up in life and love, for better or worse. This requires getting honest about the patterns of relating to ourselves and others that we've inherited from our cultures, our families, and our parents and their parents before them. It also requires getting honest about the patterns of relating to ourselves and others that we are *choosing* each day, whether consciously or unconsciously.

For so many of us (amongst women *and* men), we are acting out behavioral patterns inherited from our transgenerational survival modes, from our cultural and religious programming, from our dysfunctional families and homes of origin, and from our unhealed wounds and unacknowledged traumas.

As women, once we reach a space of foundational honesty related to our conscious and unconscious patterns (which include how we interact with the men in our lives, as well as with our friends and other loved ones), then we can carefully and humbly sit with our true underlying motivations behind *why* we most commonly prefer—and consciously choose and idealize—performing femininity over embodying femininity.

This process of self-honesty includes acknowledging both the inner darkness and the inner light motivating our actions. Because the truth is, there are always both darkness and light motivating our human actions, which are ultimately rooted in the *nafs*, the inner self that encompasses our body, mind, heart, and soul. For this reason, the spiritual concepts of *jihaad-un-nafs* and *tazkiyyatun-nafs*, which describe the inner battle/struggle of the self against the self, and the believer's commitment to daily purification of the soul respectively— are central to successful spiritual and emotional life in this world.

The truth is, no one's inner world is perfect, sinless, or without blemish; and every human soul is in need of healing and self-betterment. At the same time, no one's inner world is without light and goodness, as well as the potential for personal excellence, emotional growth, and spiritual transformation. Within men, the male soul's inner potential includes consciously choosing to shift from performing masculinity to embodying sincere, taqwaa-centered manhood instead. Within women, the female soul's inner potential includes consciously choosing to shift from performing femininity to embodying sincere, taqwaa-centered womanhood instead.

In this book, we tap into this inner potential by looking at the female soul's tendency to perform femininity at the expense of her emotional, mental, physical, and spiritual health. As such, the goal is to transform this self-harming tendency in women into a life of healthily embodying true femininity instead.

4
Why Most Women Perform Femininity

For the vast majority of women, myself included, their first experience with consciously living as a "feminine woman" is through performing femininity. It is only after a conscious healing journey—often sparked by personal trauma and/or through experiencing "rock bottom" in life—that we begin to process femininity as an internal state of *being* more than an external state of *doing*.

What Is Performing Femininity, Exactly?

Performing femininity is a type of anxious "doing" that is rooted in toxic self-abandonment. The origin of this emotionally damaging abandonment of self is often unresolved emotional trauma, such as unhealed childhood wounds, unacknowledged family-of-origin dysfunction, or the emotional addiction to unhealthy survival-mode patterns (e.g., patterns of relating to an authority figure that were initially adopted to stay unharmed and alive in an unsafe or unpredictable home environment).

Due to this unhealed (and often unknown or unacknowledged) emotional wounding, performative womanhood (and manhood) is rooted in a deep feeling of "lack" or feeling not enough. On a subconscious level, a woman who is performing femininity (and a man who is performing masculinity) believes *"I'm not enough as I am, so I need to put on a performance to get my needs met."*

Specifically, when we are performing femininity (or masculinity), at least one of these three subconscious messages (as coined by Marisa Peer, author of *I Am Enough*) are running the show in our lives:

- *I'm not enough.*
- *I'm too different.*
- *It's not available to me.*

In other words, thoughts and feelings like the following are occurring deep below the surface in our lives, often unconsciously:

- *I feel like I'm not enough of a "real woman" (or man) as I am, so I need to put on a show of femininity (or masculinity) in order to "earn" a person's love and secure their commitment.*

- *I feel like I'm so different from other people that I can't safely show up as I truly am, so I need to look at what "real women" (or men) do to earn and secure love and then I do the same.*

- *I feel like true, lasting love is not available to people like me, so if I have any chance at a successful relationship, I need to do and say exactly what other people tell me I must do and say; otherwise, I'll always be alone.*

Why Women (and Men) Self-Abandon

In the language of mental health, women (and men) who show up later in life in performative roles are often girls (and boys) who grew up in homes rooted in shame-based parenting. Shame-based parenting punishes authenticity that honors the child's true self, and it rewards self-abandonment that pleases the parent(s) or other caretaker, even when the child is quite obviously being harmed as a result. Consequently, the child learns that it is socially unacceptable and emotionally (and sometimes physically) unsafe to show up as her (or his) true self. In the book, *Healing the Shame that Binds You*, author and counselor, John Bradshaw says:

"The job of parents is to model. Modeling includes how to be a man or woman; how to relate intimately to another person; how to acknowledge and express emotions; how to fight fairly; how to have physical, emotional and intellectual boundaries; how to communicate; how to cope and survive life's unending problems; how to be self-disciplined; and how to love oneself and another. Shame-based parents cannot do any of these. They simply don't know how" (2005).

In other cases, a woman's toxic self-neglect is merely the result of having grown up in or having been socialized into a family, culture, or religious community that instilled in her the idea that female piety equals self-abandonment. Consequently, at the root of her performing femininity is this underlying principle of nearly all "good girl" cultures worldwide: *A female's inherent goodness (or piety) is rooted entirely in her complete and unhesitating willingness to serve and please others at the expense of herself.*

Thus, by the time a woman reaches adulthood, she most likely lives with a conscious or unconscious desire to win the love, affection, and approval of a man (or of men in general). This often begins with a conscious or unconscious motivation to please her own father (or father figure). She achieves this by saying and doing things she knows or genuinely imagines will impress her father and/or other men like her father, particularly in how well she performs the role of "good girl" in hopes of winning their approval. In marriage, this can also manifest as a woman trying to win the love and approval of her husband's relatives, especially his mother or any other loved one close to his heart.

If the woman's people-pleasing behavior that is already motivated by cultural or socio-religious expectations *also* includes childhood wounds from shame-based parenting, the woman most likely has additionally sustained a "father wound" and/or a "mother wound." This underlying wounding exacerbates her emotional addiction to self-abandonment and people-pleasing. Thus, the boundaries between the self and others becomes blurred and performing femininity in the name of winning a man's love and approval can become an obsession.

In the article entitled "8 Consequences of the Father Wound on Well-Being and Relationships," Dr. Mari Kovanen discusses this blurring of boundaries as a result of a father wound:

> "You may feel that you have to be available to everyone else all the time. Perhaps deep down you feel that to be loved by others, you cannot hold your boundary and say 'no' when something does not suit you" (AliveCounseling.com, 2024).

As a result of this father wound, a Muslim woman in particular will often become unable to draw a boundary or even consciously discern a difference between what is being demanded of her by external ideals of womanhood and what is *actually* required of her by her Creator as outlined in the Qur'an and prophetic teachings. Consequently, she performs femininity while imagining she is showing up exactly in the way that Allah Himself requires of her in this world.

5

How Muslims Islamicize Women's Self-Abandonment

When a Muslim woman performs femininity while consciously or unconsciously quite literally equating external male approval with pleasing Allah, the drive for a good "performance review" from men become religiously motivated. Even before the Muslim woman is married, this mindset takes the form of her showing up (or not showing up) in ways that she believes a "good Muslim man" would like or expect, even if this is at the expense of her own life goals and overall wellbeing. The woman is willing to engage in this level of self-sacrifice because in a Muslim woman's version of performative womanhood, evidence of a woman's spiritual goodness (or lack thereof) rests almost entirely in the mind and heart of a potential husband.

Many Muslim women (and men) defend this performative, self-sacrificing mindset in women by pointing out how Allah requires a wife to please her husband. However, the fault lines in this logic begin to show when they are reminded that Allah even *more so* requires everyone, male and female, to please and honor their parents. In this case, both men and women recognize that reasonable lines must be drawn between what a parent expects or demands of their adult son or daughter and what the man or woman desire and need for their own lives and overall wellbeing.

Otherwise, every man and woman would be religiously obligated to do literally *everything* their parents desire or demand so long as the thing itself isn't technically forbidden.

This would mean, for example, that both men and women would be compelled to marry someone they dislike, to follow the career path their parents demand, to follow the religious scholars and fiqh opinion their parents favor, and to even have as many or as few children as their parents desire. For the married Muslim man in particular, this would mean he would be additionally required to forfeit his role as head of household except insomuch as his every decision aligns with how his parents think a "good son" would behave. Obviously, this sort of extreme approach to honoring and obeying parents is both unreasonable and un-Islamic. However, many Muslims do not arrive at the same conclusion when it comes to a woman self-abandoning for the pleasure and approval of her husband (or potential husband), even when her self-sacrifice is obviously harming her mental, emotional, and physical health.

Meanwhile in Islam, even the strictest of religious scholars require that obedience to the husband does not cause a woman harm or deny her any of her rights, even if the action that she is doing (or being asked to do) isn't technically sinful or forbidden in front of Allah. As such, it is well-known that a woman has full rights to draw boundaries with regards to her own wellbeing and individual life and soul separate from her husband. For these reasons, it is standard for scholarly rulings to mention not only the avoidance of sin, but also the avoidance of harm or of violation of her rights as conditions restricting what can be reasonably asked of a woman in the name of respecting the leadership of a husband.

For example, on an online fatwa site well-known for its strict Islamic views in comparison to others, the following stipulation has been mentioned with regards to a woman following what her husband asks of her when she herself has a different opinion on the matter:

> "What the wife must do is obey her husband, unless that involves sin or will harm her or deprive her of her rights, in which case she should not obey him" (islamqa.com).

6

In Islam, a Woman's Life, Body, and Soul Are Her Own

In the prophetic Sunnah itself, the right of a wife to draw boundaries around her own individual soul, life choices, and body is well-established. However, due to the unfortunate circumstances of Muslims during these Last Days, wherein so many of us overlook obvious Islamic facts in favor of narratives that support performative womanhood and the erasure of the full humanity of women, the implications of the following three well-known personal and religious circumstances are often overlooked:

1) A Muslim man who is married to a Jewish or Christian woman is not allowed to compel her to change her religion even though the man recognizes (according to his Islamic faith) that her spiritual practice is fundamentally incorrect in front of Allah.

2) A woman who divorces her husband for no reason is accountable to Allah alone on the Day of Judgment. While the prophetic hadith that warns women against seeking a divorce for no reason is often used to *prevent* women from leaving a marriage when *someone else* feels she has no justifiable reason, the wording of the hadith clearly implies that the final decision to seek a divorce rests with the woman herself. Otherwise, she would have nothing to be accountable for in front of

Allah, as it was never her right to get a divorce in the first place.

3) A woman who, for example, uses sex as a form of manipulation and refuses to have intimate relations with her husband based on her whim alone is given a stern religious warning against this. Similar to number 2 above, the prophetic hadith mentioning how the angels themselves respond to this whimsical refusal is often used to prevent a woman from believing she *ever* has the right to refuse sexual relations. However, the stern warning itself is sufficient evidence that ultimately, a woman decides the boundaries around her body and sexual intimacy. Otherwise, there is no need for a warning to fear Allah in this regard, as the decision wouldn't have rested with her in the first place.

In other words, all adult children of Adam, whether male or female or Muslim or non-Muslim, are fully responsible for their own lives, bodies, and souls in this world. This is so much so that even when a person is quite obviously making a wrong choice, they are generally free to do so, so long as they are not committing any crime or are not obviously violating the safety or rights of another person. Then ultimately, every single one of us (male and female, Muslim and non-Muslim) will be called to account by Allah alone on the Day of Judgment with regards to how we lived out our lives on earth and how we treated our bodies and souls—and each other—while here.

7

Seeking Male Approval Can Become Self-Destructive and Addictive

"Every time I prayed *Istikhaarah* about whether or not to marry my husband," my friend said, "I felt a stronger dislike toward the idea."

Then my friend (whom I'll call Afifa) said something to me that I don't think I'll ever forget: "That's how I knew I should marry my husband. Because if I didn't and I instead chose a man I was really attracted to, I would be following my desires."

Till today, Afifa's words break my heart, because I know all too well where this thinking comes from. In performing femininity, the obligation of all Muslims (male and female) to stay away from feeding *sinful* desires is often conflated with a righteous woman's obligation to stay away from *any* desires that contradict a man's, especially if that man is (or desires to be) her husband.

Desire for Male Approval Is Stronger Than Her Desire

When a woman is performing femininity, the desire for external male approval often becomes so strong that she will consciously and *eagerly* suppress her own needs and desires in the process. She will also deliberately abandon and deny parts of her true self if she knows (or imagines) that her authenticity would displease men.

Over time, the woman becomes so adept at disowning the deepest parts of herself that self-abandonment becomes a seamless effort that she eventually does unconsciously. At this stage, her self-erasure becomes an emotional addiction that essentially tells her mind and nervous system that "less is more." In other words, the less she seeks what she actually wants or needs for own life and wellbeing, the more of a "real woman" she is.

For the Muslim woman, this addiction is made all the more problematic when she also mentally processes her self-erasure as pious sacrifice "for the sake of Allah." In this mental state, the more pangs of discomfort she feels as a result of her choices, the more her discomfort serves as proof of her own spiritual goodness as a "righteous woman." However, over time, she is unable to maintain this level of self-erasure, so she becomes overwhelmed by emotional exhaustion. Additionally, her spiritual life often begins to suffer as she becomes enveloped by feelings of spiritual emptiness, confusion, and/or frustration.

For many women, this is also the stage where both their mental and physical health begin to suffer in ways that can no longer be ignored or trivialized. Yet nearly all of this unwellness came about as a result of the woman overextending herself on the path of "righteous martyrdom" as a good wife and mother. Consequently, she becomes like the people who are so generous and giving to others that they put their own selves in extreme hardship and harm's way as a result. Not surprisingly, in the Qur'an, Allah Himself warns the human being (male and female) against this type of personal extremism:

وَلَا تَجْعَلْ يَدَكَ مَغْلُولَةً إِلَىٰ عُنُقِكَ وَلَا تَبْسُطْهَا كُلَّ ٱلْبَسْطِ فَتَقْعُدَ مَلُومًا مَّحْسُورًا ﴿٢٩﴾

50

"And do not make your hand [as] chained to your neck or extend it completely to its utmost reach and [thereby] become blameworthy and insolvent (or destitute)."
—*Al-Israa* (17:29)

Yet, for the woman whose entire identity and self-worth are rooted in overextending herself in the path of making other people's lives easier, not even the risk of her own emotional unwellness or spiritual destitution can deter her. In fact, for women whose womanhood is linked to performing femininity, pleasing men will almost always be a higher priority than being emotional well and spiritually nourished herself. Most seriously, for the Muslim woman living in this state, pleasing men becomes a higher priority than pleasing Allah.

This is why, for example, it is commonplace for "good women" to give up their rights, lower their standards, and trivialize divine mercies (e.g., a woman having her own wealth) in an effort to increase their chances of getting (and staying) married. This is because it is well-known in circles of performing femininity amongst Muslim women that the most highly praised woman is the one who looks at the rights that Allah grants her and at the divine mercies He offers her, yet she figuratively waves a hand of dismissal at it all while fixating on only one question, "What will please the man I want to marry?" And if it pleases that man for her to dismiss most (or all) of what Allah offers her, then that's what she will do—even if deep inside she wants something more for herself and her life.

In this mental space, the promises of a man are more meaningful and valuable to the woman's heart than the promises of Allah. Yet in her anxious pursuit of enjoying the promises of a man, she convinces herself that all of her

51

sacrifice (i.e., self-erasure) is proof that she has full faith in the promises of Allah. However, the reality is that, deep down, she is unwilling to sit patiently in the discomfort of faithfully trusting in the promise of Allah—because this would mean sitting patiently in the discomfort of displeasing or upsetting a man (or the collective male gaze). Even if all of her deepest desires for her life and marriage are *halaal* and potentially pleasing to Allah, she will give up every single one of them if she imagines that her pursuit of any of them *might* displease a man.

In other words, to the woman who knows (or accepts) no definition of womanhood or piety other than righteous martyrdom and performing femininity, the social and personal benefits of self-erasure are simply too great to give up, even in the face of promises of worldly goodness and blessed provision from Allah. So, even though her Creator Himself promises multiple rewards in this life and in the Hereafter to people of faith endowed with both patience and *tawakkul* (sincere trust in Him), neither of these qualities is prioritized in a woman performing femininity while pursuing marriage. She allows herself to consciously embrace these two qualities only *after* she is trapped in an unhealthy relationship, an unfortunate circumstance that she likely would not have experienced if she had embraced patience and tawakkul *before* she entered the relationship in the first place (or at all).

Tragically, in her "pious" life path of righteous martyrdom and performing femininity, the seeds of spiritual crisis were planted. As a result, it is highly likely that one day this same woman will imagine that Islam is to blame for her painful life circumstances. Yet it was Islam itself that she trivialized when she first chose it.

8
Why Performing Femininity Is So Emotionally Addictive

In an article entitled "Emotional Addiction," Dr. Mark Steinberg, PhD poses a question that is the title of an entire section called "How Can Emotions Be Addicting?" In responding to this daunting question, he says:

> "You may wonder how something inside you that's natural can be addicting. Actually, all addictions are inside you—in your brain and body…[T]he addiction is a response to intense pleasure (or relief) by repeated use of, response to, or ingestion of some behavior or substance that relieves discomfort, specifically *anxiety or pain*" (marksteinberg.com, 2024).

For a woman performing femininity, the discomfort being avoided through her emotional addiction is the fear of male rejection, displeasure, or abandonment. Specifically, she fears showing up in any way except what will clearly earn her male validation, pleasure, and approval. So, her self-erasure (which is an inherent trait of performative womanhood) becomes a means to alleviate the anxiety that would arise if she doesn't get a "good performance review" from the male gaze. Additionally, her emotional self-abandonment (which is at the heart of performing femininity) protects her from the pain of the male rejection, displeasure or abandonment that would occur if she were to show up as her full self.

Consequently, in her internal world, she begins to rely on the flood of positive emotions that wash over her in the form of the relief she experiences once she gets that "good job" from the male gaze. This internal feeling of profound relief and immediate removal of anxiety is at the root of all addictions, including emotional addictions. Dr. Steinberg says:

> "In the case of emotions, the response is a reliance upon and absorption in the brain and neurological patterns that produce a flood of feelings... You become 'addicted' to the substance or action that subdues anxiety, but at great cost and with counterproductive effects" (2024).

Though there is a high price to pay for this "emotional drug" (in both the short-term and the long-term), the social and personal benefits are simply too high to give up performative womanhood altogether, as aforementioned. As a result, the woman remains emotionally addicted to the "high" of feeling like a "good woman"—or of being celebrated as a "righteous woman" who represents the very essence of female piety. So, she continues to overstretch herself on this path of self-erasure and self-abandonment. Then her inner world becomes "hooked" on the inner pull of good feelings she experiences for a "job well done" on the stage of performative womanhood. Dr. Steinberg says:

> "In the case of emotional addiction, you become 'hooked' either on feeling a familiar way or in responding in an automatic way to the powerful pull of innate emotions. Emotional addicts pay heavily for their fixes, though not in dollars to a dealer. The cost of emotional addiction is that you live at the mercy of feelings provoked by circumstances (whether initiated by happenstance or foreordained by unconsciously imprinted negatively

scripted behavior) and your perceptions of these events. The overpowering feelings transcend other brain responses, and you need to make sensible decisions, rather than react to impulses" (2024).

In women emotionally addicted to performing femininity, amongst the brain responses that are being transcended in this performance for the male gaze are the ever-deepening messages:

- *I'm not worthy.*
- *I'm not enough.*
- *My needs and desires aren't important.*
- *I don't matter.*
- *Something is deeply wrong with me as I am.*

In other words, every time a woman self-abandons at the cost of nurturing her own wellness, desires, or needs—which is completely different from making the conscious decision to participate in a healthy compromise or personal sacrifice that is soul-nourishing—she feeds a subconscious mental programming of internalized self-hate. As a result, making sensible decisions for herself or her life becomes nearly impossible. Instead, her entire life becomes one big performance after the other, each one incited by the impulse to please others at the expense of herself.

9

The Making of a "Good Woman"

The last time I spoke to my friend Afifa, she was seeking a divorce from her abusive husband and had literally escaped from him and from her own family out of fear for her life and safety. Today she looks back at those moments when she repeatedly prayed *Istikhaarah* before marriage and is stunned at how she completely misread the warning signs from Allah.

On the outside looking in, it's easy for us to think, "Well, obviously she shouldn't have married him if she didn't want to!" However, so very many of us as women fall into a similar trap when we don't even *perceive*, let alone misread, the warnings signs from Allah. And here, I'm talking about the warning signs that He has placed within our own *nafs* in the form of intuition. However, because so many of us have completely internalized our own self-erasure, we don't even *detect* when our inner world is saying no. And if we do detect that inner no, we often don't honor it (because we don't feel we have the right to). Unfortunately, a large part of this is due to the fact that, in performing femininity, women are routinely shamed away from self-love. As a result, they adopt its destructive opposite, even if only unconsciously.

Abandoning Self-Love and Internalizing Self-Hate

Tragically, the internalized self-hate of women suffering from the self-destructive emotional addiction of performing femininity often goes undetected for years or even for generations. This is often because in "good girl" cultures, it is entirely socially acceptable (and sometimes even actively encouraged) for women to hate themselves. Why? Because so long as a woman's self-loathing wins the "love" and approval of men, then it is deemed good and praiseworthy.

As a result, the most radiant parts of a woman's unique, divinely gifted personality are dulled or snuffed out in the conscious or unconscious attempt at pleasing men and never appearing "un-feminine" to them. This carefully crafted self-erasure is how so many women position themselves as the prototypical "feminine woman."

As a feminine prototype, the woman is now "wife material" and thus worthy of being chosen (and kept) as a man's partner for life. This step-by-step process of crafting oneself to fit into a very specific external ideal of a "good woman" is the very essence of performing femininity.

This externally focused performative behavior makes the experience of true, soul-nourishing love nearly impossible in a woman's life (and also in the life of the man who married her), as will be discussed in Part Two in detail. This impossibility is mainly due to the fact that so long as a woman is performing femininity, there is a necessary prerequisite (or "price of entry") that requires disconnection over connection.

As a result, true intimacy (or even consistently deeply felt sensual pleasure) is unattainable in that performative relationship, as there will always be an invisible wall between the woman and herself and thus an invisible wall between the woman and her husband. Yet true intimacy and sensual connection can never occur when one or both people are hiding from themselves, or are hiding themselves from the other.

PART TWO
TEN REASONS
Why Performing Femininity Never Works in Love

"Every human soul, male and female, and every human relationship, platonic and romantic, has both darkness and light. When we are unhealed, we can tolerate only a small amount of light within ourselves and in a relationship. So, we play victim or savior to feel we've chosen more light than we actually have. But deep down we're terrified of truly stepping into our light—and of supporting our loved one truly stepping into theirs."
—from the journal of Umm Zakiyyah

REASON ONE
True Love Requires Authenticity

"I now see how owning our story and loving ourselves through that process is the bravest thing that we will ever do."
—Brené Brown

"The act of performing is just that, it's an act. It means you're not being authentic. But so many of us learned in early childhood that being authentic and being 'good' could never coexist—at least not within a girl."
—from the journal of Umm Zakiyyah

10

A Good Girl Learning to Be Good

From my earliest memories of childhood, anxious people-pleasing defined my existence. It wasn't until my late thirties that I began to even process the meaning of self-care. After that, it took several more years for me to understand the meaning and necessity of self-love. But it wasn't until after my second divorce, when I was in my forties, that the concept of feeling emotionally safe held any meaning or significance for me at all.

Raised in the "tough love" environment that defined so many good families trying to protect their children from the horrors of racism and varying degrees of cruelty in the "real world," I came to live in fear, anxiety, and hypervigilance as a state of being. Growing up, I relied on all three aspects of this inner emotional state. Ultimately, I began to see each aspect as a necessary mechanism for survival and for existing with any reasonable semblance of safety in this world.

When I was navigating the world outside my home; fear, anxiety, and hypervigilance kept me on high alert whenever I was in a potentially hostile environment, such as in American public school, where I was routinely bullied as a Muslim girl—even as teachers and administrators looked on, not intervening. When I was navigating the world inside my home; fear, anxiety, and hypervigilance kept me out of trouble with my parents (at least for the most part), who accepted only complete and total obedience from me and my siblings. As is common in tough love (even with the best of intentions and the most compassionate of parents), we were not allowed to show even the slightest sign of *feeling* upset about anything we were told. This insistence on obeying without thought, backtalk, or inner resistance was, for the most part, my parents' sincere attempt to prepare us for the "real world" and to protect us from its harsh realities at the same time.

However, the unintended side effect of this tough-love approach on my psyche was threefold (though I would not have the words for these feelings until much later in life):

1) I went through my childhood and young adulthood feeling that nothing I felt or thought mattered.
2) I went through childhood and young adulthood feeling that *I* didn't matter.
3) I went through childhood and young adulthood feeling that nowhere was safe to authentically exist in this world, not even my own home.

Consequently, I learned to shift between showing no weakness and showing no strength, depending on whichever external façade granted me one or more of these outcomes: (1) the deepest sense of safety, (2) the highest likelihood of being protected from harm, and (3) the greatest chance of enjoying some semblance of acceptance, love, or praise from those more powerful (and thus more important) than me. So, at school I showed no weakness, and at home I showed no strength.

At school the slightest sign of weakness was effectively an invitation for harm, and at home the slightest sign of strength (which was often perceived as defiance or disrespect) was effectively an invitation for punishment. The only thing that earned me safety in both environments—in the form of praise, acceptance, or invisibility—was getting a good "performance review" from "the boss." In each environment, "the boss" was whoever was most powerful and thus running the show and making all the rules.

In this way, my entire life turned into a huge performance act wherein I eagerly auditioned for the coveted role of having the right to exist in peace.

11
Who's the Boss?

"Children learn quickly that they must shift who they are depending on where they are—just as they saw modeled—in order to survive and be loved."
—Dr. Nicole LePara, *How to Do the Work: Recognize Your Patterns, Heal from Your Past, and Create Your Self*

In the hallways of public school, "the boss" was the popular crowd who praised, accepted, or overlooked you only if you blended in with them (thus granting you invisibility). If you could also pull off being distinctly attractive and "cool" according to their standards—but never so much as to outshine them—then all the better.

In the classrooms of public school, "the boss" was the teachers who praised and accepted only good grades and "good behavior," which meant sitting quietly still and attentive as they spoke. And so long as the teachers themselves were never the target of any calculated student harm, they generally turned a blind eye to any wrongdoing happening in front of them. That is, they intervened only when they feared that their non-intervention would get them in trouble with higher-up administrators. So, I learned to endure all manners of bullying (e.g., physical assault, verbal abuse, and sexual harassment) as par for the course in a typical school day—without even the *hope* of being helped, supported, or protected by the adults officially assigned to these roles.

At home "the boss" was my father, who was an authoritarian in every sense of the word (verbally and physically), as was standard in homes of "good families" rooted in tough love. Meanwhile, my mother, though softer in temperament and heart, was his unwavering, dedicated assistant who kept a watchful (albeit more compassionate) eye on us whenever he was not around. My mother, ever the dedicated wife, never faltered in holding us to every one of my father's strict rules and physical punishments, even in moments when it took everything in her to *not* show mercy on our behalf.

As a result of these collective experiences, my life throughout my youth became a delicate balance of seeking praise and acceptance by "the boss" at home and school. And whenever that wasn't possible, I learned to walk on eggshells so as to at least stay out of harm's way. In this way, I learned to effectively shapeshift for the purpose of safety and survival—and for the ever-elusive hope of acceptance and love.

12

The Overachiever of Survival Mode

Thankfully, I survived each environment unscathed, at least for the most part—with the added bonus of a long list of overachievement accolades each year.

At school, I earned multiple rewards from teachers and administrators (officially and socially) for my high academic achievements and for displaying impeccably good behavior. I even earned a few rewards from fellow students (officially and socially) for being cool (at times).

At home, I earned high praise for being a model "good girl" who almost always obeyed her parents and who went over and beyond in making them proud. Additionally, in my religious community, I earned high praise for being a model "good Muslim" who was known to consistently put her faith first and to almost always do "the right thing."

However, by the time I was a teenager, I felt myself becoming increasingly exhausted and longing for escape from it all. Deep inside, I just wanted to relax, to rest, and to be myself.

I just wanted to be *free*.

By the time I was sixteen years old and a senior in high school, I started counting down to the day I could make my freedom a reality—and I had a bona fide escape plan. This plan involved two simple steps (at least I *thought* they were simple at the time):

(1) Leave home and go to college.

(2) Craft an entirely new life for myself through meeting my "forever love" and getting married.

Little did I know, marriage would become just one more life stage where putting on a good performance was more valuable than showing up as my unique, complex, authentic self.

RE-CAP

Reason 1

Why Performing Femininity Never Works in Love

●━━━━━━━━━━━━━━━━●

True love requires authenticity.
This means showing up as your true self.
However, performing femininity requires
showing up while performing an "act" that has
been scripted for you.

Compassionate Accountability Prompts
for Embodying Femininity

1. In the beginning of this section, I describe myself in
   childhood as "a good girl trying to be good." This led
   to anxious people-pleasing that disconnected me
   from my own thoughts, desires, and feelings. **Think
   back to your earliest memories of childhood.
   How would you describe how you *felt* at this
   time?** Did these early-life feelings incite anxiousness,
   insecurity, people-pleasing, and/or hypervigilance?
   How so?

   I emphasize the word *felt* above for this reason: We
   can know on an intellectual level that we were loved
   and appreciated by our parents (or other caretakers)
   but still recall *feeling* unloved and unseen. While it's
   praiseworthy to acknowledge what you *know to be true*

in your mind, it is ultimately how you *felt inside about yourself* that determines how you show up later in life, especially in marriage and other relationships.

2. In this section, I also mention how the unintended side effect of my own tough-love upbringing was threefold:

   ✓ I went through my childhood and young adulthood feeling that nothing I felt or thought mattered.

   ✓ I went through my childhood and young adulthood feeling that *I* didn't matter.

   ✓ I went through my childhood and young adulthood feeling that nowhere was safe to authentically exist in this world, not even my own home.

   Do you recognize yourself or your "inner child" in any of these feelings? If so, how so? Or perhaps you recognize the *opposite* of any of these feelings? If so, how so? For example, if your parents heavily relied on you for adult tasks (e.g., taking care of their other children) or unhealthily confided in you as a child, then you might have felt the opposite of what I felt growing up: Perhaps you felt that *everything* you felt and thought mattered, because your parents (or caretakers) were incapable or unwilling to feel and think for themselves. Or they were incapable or unwilling to take accountability for their own thoughts and feelings, so they relied on yours.

3. Which of the following words most closely capture how you felt deep inside growing up? **Choose one or more of the following words that incite even the *tiniest* flicker of inner recognition inside you.** And here, be careful to avoid trivializing, dismissing, or explaining away any of your inner feelings:

68

unloved	unseen	unsafe
unwanted	unappreciated	terrified
"ugly"	angry or sad	overwhelmed
"bad"	neglected	hypervigilant

If any one or more of the above words resonate with you, write a letter to your younger self, saying:

> *Dear* _____ (using your childhood name or a nickname that is closest to your heart),
> *I'm sorry you felt*_____. *I wish* _____. *Please know* _____. *And know, I'm here for you now, and I'm not going to leave you ever again.*

The letter can be as long or as short as you like. If you prefer, speak aloud these words instead of writing them down. You might also choose to record this letter via audio or a voice note. As you write or speak this letter to your younger self, feel free to alter any of the wording until it feels most authentic for you.

REASON TWO
Love Is About Being Fully Seen,
Performing Is About Hiding

"An unseen woman hardens, a seen woman naturally blooms."
—Philip Attar

"Performing femininity asks women to suppress, give up, or disconnect from parts of themselves in exchange for male approval."
—from the journal of Umm Zakiyyah

13

Perfecting the Art of Being Invisible

At sixteen years old, what exhausted me most was that none of my original bosses, at home or school, seemed to *see* me. So, while I was heavily praised and rewarded for showing meekness at home (through being humbly obedient and non-confrontational to my parents) and for showing strength at school (through being a cool, feisty, and "cute" academic), the need to constantly both stay out of harm's way and upset no one meant that it was never safe to be myself, that it was never safe to be fully *seen*.

I had to be on my best behavior at all times (according to the rules laid down by "the bosses"), and the slightest deviance from this "straight and narrow" was punished severely. This meant that five things were out of the question at both home and school:

(1) showing evidence of having deep emotional needs unique to my own inner world, as this could be perceived as seeking "special attention" at home and an invitation for bullying at school

(2) showing the slightest sign of disagreement with anyone more powerful or more important than me (i.e., any of "the bosses"), as this almost always ended in getting into trouble or putting myself in harm's way

(3) showing the slightest sign of genuine confusion as to why things had to be a certain way, as this almost

always led to others' questioning my loyalty, trustworthiness, or sincerity

(4) having desires or goals that either contradicted the bosses' or that did not align with their desires or goals for me or themselves, as this (for fairly obvious reasons) was a recipe for trouble

(5) freely exploring what I truly desired for myself and my life, as this put me at risk of being ostracized, socially isolated, or punished

The unwritten rule in all of these environments was that my role as a nonperson was to serve the bosses' interests and goals at all times. This meant that I was never allowed to stand out as an individual personality. However, regarding this latter point, there was one caveat: If I displayed unique talents and abilities that could be used to amplify the bosses' interests and goals, then my individual personality was not only accepted, it was celebrated.

In other words, my greatest chance at being seen and appreciated as a unique individual soul in the world was to make myself both incredibly useful and incredibly invisible at the same time.

14
Getting to Know My New Bosses

As it turned out, my escape plan toward freedom—through leaving home and going to college, and then meeting my "forever love" and getting married—just landed me in the same circumstances I'd sought escape from. To my surprise, these two new environments held fast to the same rules that had incited the suffocating, self-suppression that defined my childhood and youth.

In the end, I came to this sober conclusion: What felt to me like I was disappearing from existence so that other "more important" people could live more freely and thus more happily and more fulfilled, was precisely what was most valued in me in both college and marriage.

As a Muslim student at a predominately Christian, "liberal arts" university, I was expected to shrink and disappear in significance next to my non-Muslim professors and classmates and to conform to their Islamophobic mindsets. Similarly, as a Muslim woman seeking to be a "righteous wife" in marriage, I was expected to shrink and disappear in significance next to my husband. Additionally, in the wider Muslim community, I was expected to conform to the general anti-women cultural mindset, which disapproved of any woman standing out—except in becoming an overachiever in self-abandonment.

Ultimately, my heart fell in submission to what I perceived as my *qadar*, my divinely assigned fate: *This is the path to Paradise,* I told myself. *If you're patient as you shrink and disappear yourself from existence, you'll not only be safe and non-threatening as a Muslim woman in the United States of America, but you'll also be loved and appreciated as a Muslim wife in marriage. You'll also be a valuable member of the universal Muslim community. Then, most importantly, you'll be loved and appreciated by Allah.*

During this time of patient servitude—which required continuous, self-inflicted emotional suffering (at least in the way I myself understood "patient servitude" at the time)—I was routinely spoken about (and to) as an example of what a "good Muslim woman" looked like and how a "righteous wife" behaved. Consequently, I was appreciated and celebrated most by my brothers and sisters in faith during the time in my life when I loved and honored myself the least.

Neither they nor I was consciously or intentionally engaging in the celebration of my self-abandonment. We just genuinely imagined that we were all doing (and celebrating) the "right things."

15

Enduring It All for the Sake of Allah

For years, I carried on in a mental state that I now call "righteous martyrdom." This is an inner emotional and spiritual state maintained by a person who imagines that her (or his) self-erasure and continuous self-abandonment are for some elusive, blessed "greater good." However, in reality, this person's inner world mirrors the deflated spirit of a prisoner of war or of a woman (or man) sold into human trafficking who has given up all hopes of freedom, happiness, or escape.

During this difficult time, I survived each moment and each day only by telling myself that I was living the life of a "righteous woman." I told myself that this life of endless sacrifice, of continuously shrinking myself for the sake of my husband, and of maintaining invisibility (and thus non-personage) in my Muslim community were what God required of pious women in life, marriage, and faith.

Before I decided to dissolve my marriage in the hopes of salvaging some semblance of my emotional and spiritual wellness, there were times that I tried really, really hard *not* to give up on this path of piety. In these moments, I would suppress my emotional pain and quiet my incessant doubts by saying aloud over and over, sometimes in a daze of mental exhaustion while mindlessly completing household chores: *"You are nothing but a slave. You are nothing but a slave."* And by this humiliating terminology, I did *not* mean a slave of Allah. I meant a slave to my husband.

Even after I sought divorce (again) in my second marriage, I felt the ever-increasing pressures of being a "good Muslim woman" as defined by the collective male gaze. I would later learn that these social pressures that I mistook for female piety went far beyond anything definitively required of me by the Qur'an or prophetic teachings. But at the time I was sacrificing myself on the altar of righteous martyrdom, I genuinely imagined that this level of self-erasure was indeed required of me by my Creator and praised by His Messenger (peace be upon him).

16

The Sin of Being Seen or Heard

To add insult to injury, during the time in my life when I was suffering the most emotionally and spiritually—and trying so hard to hold on to my *emaan* (Islamic faith)—so many in the Muslim community (amongst men *and* women) felt that it was both their right and religious obligation to micromanage, criticize, and find fault in every single aspect of a woman's existence.

In my faith community, they called this daily harassment of women "commanding the good and forbidding the evil." Or to put it in the language of American culture, they viewed their daily harassment of women as "doing God's work." In this mental space, they often also assigned themselves the praiseworthy label of being "on the right path." Other times, they simply labeled their attacks on women as fighting "the evil influences" of corrupt Western ideology and "feminism."

If the woman being attacked or criticized was in the public space, especially on social media, the micromanaging, criticizing, and fault-seeking reached epidemic proportions. This was the case even if her entire public role was in something spiritually beneficial like *da'wah* (teaching others about Islam) or sharing inspirational reflections from the Qur'an. In this space, a woman need not be guilty of actual sin or wrongdoing to become the target of calculated harm. She need only to arouse the slightest suspicions, doubt, irritation, or *"fitnah"* in the heart of any random person, especially a man, who happened to be observing her.

This female transgression could include a "violation" as simple as following a *fiqh* opinion that the observer disagreed with. For example, if a woman was doing any of the following three things, she could find herself the target of vicious verbal attacks and character assassination: reciting the Qur'an in front of an audience of both women and men, wearing hijab that displayed her face and hands in public (i.e., not covering her *entire* body, literally), or merely *speaking* to her own dedicated female audience via audio or video but in a space that men also had access to it.

Or she could simply show up as a divorced woman who wasn't obviously distraught and depressed or desperate for remarriage. If she went a step further and offered to coach or support other women healing from divorce, the attacks intensified.

Meanwhile, these Muslims consistently defended their behavior by citing the prophetic hadith that obligates anyone who sees an evil to remove it with their hands or tongues. However, what these Muslims failed to understand was the implication at the very foundation of that prophetic instruction: Any evil (or good) you see in someone has much more to do with the state of your own heart and mind than with any actual evil (or good) in the person you're observing. This is because, as the Qur'an teaches us, we see with our hearts more than our eyes.

17

We See with Our Hearts, Not Our Eyes

"I've been on this journey since 2018 [of overcoming being so judgmental and critical of others], and before that I really suffered for most of my life," the woman said.

She then explained that it was only through learning self-love that she was able to see others more compassionately and stop seeing so many their faults. "I did journaling… reading… [and] therapy," she explains. "[I learned] about CPTSD and… finally acknowledging my trauma… [and] understanding my family dynamic." She also shared how she grew up in what she calls a "shaming culture" and then as she healed, she refused to continue living like this. She also said:

> "In regards to criticism, I can say that the family environment I grew up in was very critical and that my dad was critical towards most people… I grew up feeling watched all time, very afraid, very cautious, and so harsh on myself when I made mistakes or when I didn't behave like I was supposed to. So my criticism was a way for me to not get into that position where I would be 79criticized by my dad, mom or sister or by others. It was self-protection really. I became immune to my harsh criticism so when I dished it to others, I didn't consider the impact since I was numb to it. But mostly it was towards myself, my self-esteem was low and I was oscillating between

feelings of inferiority and superiority. Judging others makes you feel superior, so in a way it makes you feel better about yourself, but not really…" (Reddit.com r/CPTSD, 2023).

Hurt Hearts Hurt People

When our own hearts are hurting, wounded, or unwell, we see the world through that lens. It's not something we do on purpose; it is simply how the human world of perception operates within the mind and *nafs*, especially if we are living with symptoms of CPTSD (complex post-traumatic stress disorder)—or complex post-traumatic stress injury (i.e., a PTSD-like emotional injury or wounding)—which happens as a result of childhood trauma amongst other things.

It's like the saying, *"A person can only spend from what he has."* Therefore, whatever condition our minds, hearts, and *nafs* are in will *always* be the foundation of the "reality" we perceive around us and within us, and it will always be the filter through which we process everything and everyone else in the world, for better or worse.

If that foundational reality is rooted in unhealed wounds, we will likely be harshly critical of others and then justify it through whatever worldview we have, be it religion, "keepin' it real," or seeing ourselves as "truth tellers." What helps to overcome the tendency to be harshly critical of others is to heal our hearts. This requires humbly learning from others and their life journeys (and from our own).

Being a humble student of life and the world around us allows us to learn wisdom. Only then we can hear what is *truly* being said and actually see what is *truly* in front of us, instead of seeing merely dark shadows that we cast on others from our inner world.

In the Qur'an, Allah says:

أَفَلَمْ يَسِيرُوا فِي ٱلْأَرْضِ فَتَكُونَ لَهُمْ قُلُوبٌ يَعْقِلُونَ بِهَآ أَوْ ءَاذَانٌ يَسْمَعُونَ بِهَا ۖ فَإِنَّهَا لَا تَعْمَى ٱلْأَبْصَـٰرُ وَلَـٰكِن تَعْمَى ٱلْقُلُوبُ ٱلَّتِي فِي ٱلصُّدُورِ ﴿٤٦﴾

"Do they not travel through the land, so that their hearts may thus learn wisdom and their ears may thus learn to hear? Truly it is not their eyes that are blind, but their hearts which are in their breasts."
—*Al-Hajj* (22:46)

During my own personal journey, it wouldn't be until many years after experiencing continuous harassment, verbal abuse, and fault-seeking in the name of *"Whoever of you sees an evil should remove it..."* in my faith community that I had this epiphany, which I noted as a personal reflection in my journal:

We see with our hearts more than our eyes. So, whenever a person consistently sees evil in others, their attempts to remove that evil isn't necessarily about removing an actual evil that exists in that person. Rather, it is more so about them responding to the unhealthy state of their own heart, which incites them to continuously project their own inner darkness onto others.

And if we're honest with ourselves, we will realize that we too have the tendency to fall into this, especially when we find ourselves *consistently* seeing the "sinful" or "toxic" behavior of others and then constantly feeling "obligated" to call it out, fix it, or make *them* see how wrong they are.

18

Harming Others for the Sake of Allah

For years, I repeatedly suffered health issues as a result of many Muslims' self-proclaimed "commanding the good and forbidding the evil," especially when the fault-seeking reached the level of public and private slander, as it so often did. Yet still, these Muslims felt that what they were doing was "for the sake of Allah," which is a common Islamic phrase that, as alluded to earlier, effectively means "doing the Lord's work."

Till today, I struggle to make sense of how so many ostensibly good Muslims (amongst men and women) feel like they're earning good deeds while they consistently and persistently make women feel unsafe, unwanted, and "less than" in our community spaces—even when she is guilty of no apparent sin or wrongdoing. For example, a woman merely seeking a divorce or having what others consider "high standards" for marriage subjects her to this type of harm.

"It feels like I'm in an abusive relationship that I can't get out of," I said once to a friend while describing how I felt trying to hold on to my faith as a Muslim woman in such a hostile, intolerant intra-religious environment.

It took nearly losing my life and faith, along with receiving a compassionate but firm warning from my doctor, before I took an honest look at myself and my life. In this life-changing moment, I began a critical examination of the choices I was repeatedly making in the name of faith, family, and love. Before then, I didn't even fully process that the ways I was showing up were conscious choices. I just saw them as the unavoidable "realities of life."

At the time, I genuinely imagined I had no other choice except to keep "sacrificing for the sake of Allah," which for me really just meant continuously putting everything and everyone "more important" before myself. That is, I believed I had no other choice but to continue on this path if I wanted to be counted as a good person, a righteous woman, or a companion of Paradise.

RE-CAP

Reason 2
Why Performing Femininity Never Works in Love

●————————————————————————●

Love is about being fully seen and heard.
Performing femininity, on the other hand, is
about hiding and suppressing your voice.

Compassionate Accountability Prompts
for Embodying Femininity

1. In the beginning of this section, I discuss how as a teenager, I perfected "the art of being invisible." **Think back to how you felt during your early childhood and/or teenage years.** Did you feel like you needed to hide who you really are to be loved and accepted? Did you feel pressured to hide your thoughts and feelings to protect others (or yourself)? Or did you *wish* you could make yourself invisible and insignificant somehow? Perhaps because the adults in your life relied too heavily on you or because your boundaries were being constantly violated?

   If any of these feelings or thoughts resonate with you, look deep within and answer honestly: **In your relationships today, how do you find yourself carrying out these roles of invisibility, of trying to "disappear" to stay safe, or of carrying other** people's burdens at the expense of yourself? Where do you wish you could feel more seen, cherished, and accepted for who you *really* are, and not just for the benefit or convenience of someone else? Where do you wish you could just be left alone and not relied on so much?

2. **Have you ever felt the need to suffer or remain in perpetual misery as a show of piety, patience, or feminine goodness?** If so, how so? In your opinion and estimation, where did you first learn these ideas of piety, patience, and feminine goodness? Or perhaps you still hold on to these ideas today? If so, why? Do you think there is *also* room for deeply felt joy and inner contentment? Why or why not?

3. **Take in a deep breath and exhale slowly until you are in a space of mental calm.** If you like, place a hand on your chest until you can feel your heartbeat. Then read these words aloud in a gentle voice while fully taking them in: *Dear beautiful soul, it's okay to not be okay. And it's also okay to embrace joy and contentment for the sake of Allah.*

4. When you think about your life, your relationships, and the world around you, **do you generally feel optimistic and hopeful, even in the face of obvious challenges and trials? Or do you generally feel stressed, distressed, angry, resentful, frustrated, or overwhelmed?** (And here, the operative word is *generally*. As human beings with a wide range of feelings, it is only natural to *sometimes* feel optimistic and hopeful, and to also *sometimes* feel stressed, distressed, angry, resentful, frustrated, or overwhelmed. However, it is how we feel most of the time that gives us a pretty good idea of where we are *generally*).

If you generally feel optimistic and hopeful, what comes to your mind and heart that allows you to feel this way? If you generally feel pessimistic (e.g., distressed, angry, resentful, etc.), **what unhealed emotional pain or childhood wound do you think is beneath the surface of these perpetual dark feelings?**

5. If you're often on social media and you'd like to begin to see the world around you with a better, more radiant part your heart (instead of through the darkest, hurting part of your heart), try this:

Do a social media "soul cleanse." This means using every moment you spend online as an opportunity to benefit to your spiritual life, *bi'idhnillaah*. How? In addition to seeking out and sharing posts that are beneficial reminders to yourself and others, interact with others in a way that helps purify your heart from anything that can sully your soul. Also, interact with others in a way that helps true love for the sake of Allah take root in your heart.

Here's what I find helpful: Honor your guests, whether they enter your personal space virtually, in reality, or in your thoughts. Pray for them. Ask Allah to bless them and grant them happiness and the highest success in this world and in the Hereafter.

If you see someone falling into error or sin, ask Allah to guide them and forgive them. If someone is posting about their own happiness and success, take a moment to leave a comment congratulating them and praying for Allah's blessings for them and for them being increased in good.

And whenever you have a free moment, take time to send someone a message to just ask how they are doing, or to just send your love and salaams, especially if you aren't close friends who interact often.

REASON THREE
Performing Asks Women to Show Up Empty, Love Asks Women to Show Up Full

—————————●————————————●—————————

"I believe we can nurture love, but we cannot create it. As humans, we can only grow love from a seed of openness that is already there. Only Allah has the power to create something from nothing."
—from the journal of Umm Zakiyyah

"You can be the most beautiful person in the world and everybody sees light and rainbows when they look at you, but if you yourself don't know it, all of that doesn't even matter."
—C. JoyBell C.

19

The Boy at the Skating Rink

When I was sixteen years old and in my last year of high school, my sister and I went to a local skating rink one evening. Our father dropped us off. I remember being so excited, as I usually was whenever I had the opportunity to go skating with my sister. She was about a year younger than I was and was also my best friend.

My sister and I must have roller-skated for a solid two or three hours, trying to soak up as much of the window of time allotted for that night's skate session. When we finished, I remember that heady feeling of joy and satisfaction as I removed my rental skates and made my way toward the skate-return counter. As I passed the cluster of lockers where people often left their personal belongings while they skated, I happened to see a boy I knew from school (whom I'll call Nathan). I immediately recognized Nathan from my early morning homeroom and physics class.

As Nathan's gaze met mine, I saw in his expression that he recognized me too, and a hint of a smile formed on his face. Instinctively, I smiled and waved, saying, "Oh hey, Nathan." He said hey to me too, and I remember feeling a bit flattered that he even knew my name.

I then proceeded to go meet up my sister who had been several strides ahead of me. But just as I began to move forward, Nathan came toward me, but in a way that incited confusion and discomfort. I smiled awkwardly and paused in case he wanted to tell me something. That was when I noticed the slight stumble in his walk and his watery red eyes. My heart dropped. I had never been around alcohol in my home, but in that moment, I remember realizing without a shadow of doubt: *Oh my God, he's drunk.*

My heart raced as I started to back away from him, but with each step I took backward, Nathan stumbled toward me. He spoke to me with slightly slurred speech, but his words were clear in their expression of his physical attraction toward me and a desire for the feeling to be mutual. Yet the words he was saying to me and about me were so inappropriate that they made my skin crawl.

As I continued to back away from him, I mentally gauged my surroundings to see if there was any easy escape. But I felt cornered in the space I had backed into at the lockers and was beginning to feel trapped. Meanwhile, I masked my wariness by smiling and saying whatever flattering words I could think of while also refusing his advances. My intention was to let Nathan know that I wasn't interested in a relationship with him but that I still considered him to be a good person. But he didn't seem to register any of this.

He kept stumbling toward me and making inappropriate remarks, and I kept backing away while verbally refusing as best I could, an awkward, apologetic smile plastered to my face. However, the look in Nathan's eyes was of a person who was not fully present, so nothing I was saying was getting through to him. Around us, there was the loud din of other skaters talking and laughing deeply engrossed in their own conversations faded in the background. I felt completely alone.

Terrified for my safety, I panicked inside and began using firmer words of refusal. When that didn't work and he came so close to me that I feared he would put his hands on me, my mind went crazy in desperation. Then I screamed, "Get away from me, you lowlife!"

Nathan froze in front of me, and his watery red eyes looked at me in a mixture of shock and rage. It was the first time I saw any sign of life in his gaze, but it was the type of "life" that gave me chills. I stared back at him, feeling just as shocked as he did by my screaming and by the offensive word that I'd used to jolt him into the present. A split second later, I realized this was my opportunity to escape, so I hurried away from him, still shaken by the exchange.

About a minute later I met up with my sister outside in front of the skating rink, and when we saw our father pull up near the curb, we climbed into the car. On the car ride home, though I talked lightheartedly with my sister, I felt unsettled and ashamed, like I'd done something terrible that I could never live down.

That night I had a sick feeling in my stomach and was overcome with trepidation that I had gone too far in how I spoke to Nathan. I feared he would never forget it. But I hung on to a thread of hope that he was too drunk to remember anything.

I was wrong.

The next school day, right as I walked into homeroom before our physics class, Nathan glared at me and said, "B**ch, I might've been drunk, but I remember what you said." He then vowed that he would make my life hell every single day for the rest of the year.

And he did.

This included name-calling, expressing violent fantasies of inflicting harm on me, and verbal abuse that was so sexually graphic that I felt terrified and physically sick every time I crossed his path. Meanwhile teachers and students looked on in silence, and I felt as if there was a camaraderie amongst them that manifested in a unified voice of somber conviction: *Don't intervene. She deserves every single horrible thing that's happening to her.*

Some days that somber voice was my own.

20

An Empty Vessel and Blank Slate?

Till today, I'm working through the emotional wounding of living through over hundred days of Nathan's verbal abuse and sexual harassment day after day during my last year of high school—and till today, there is a part of me that still blames myself.

Not too long ago, I mentioned this painful experience to a Muslim male psychotherapist, and during our Zoom session, he appeared quite bored with my story. He was toying with his beard the entire time, and that's where his gaze was lazily fixed. It was only when I got to the part of the story where I screamed at Nathan and called him a "lowlife" that the therapist began paying attention. He paused his hair pulling, stared at me with eyes wide, and sucked in his breath in shock, saying only, "Wow."

When I shared how Nathan harassed me day after day and used sexually graphic language to torment me, the therapist sort of shrugged, as if to say, "Well, that tracks. You went too far in how you reacted to him, so of course he's going to take out his anger on you."

In that moment, I felt as if even this therapist was saying: *As a woman, you have to accept that men will harass you and make you fear for your life and safety. That's just a normal part of life. But as a woman, it is never acceptable for you to refuse a man's advances or protect yourself from harm in a way that wounds his ego, offends his honor, or makes him angry. If you do, that makes your behavior exponentially worse than his.* I know that this therapist wasn't consciously intending to convey this hurtful message, but it was the one I received, nonetheless.

Moreover, later in life I would receive a variant of this same message in how the wounded masculine expected a woman to respond to a man's advances or to his desire for a relationship with her or even for marriage itself. If she was a "good woman" living in her femininity, she was expected to have almost no boundaries, no standards, and no fears of her own—at least not if any of these conflicted with a man's desire to have her for himself. Because of this very well-known and often widely accepted notion of feminine goodness, Muslim women living in performative womanhood often respond to a proposal of marriage in the same way they would to an intimidating man flirting with them on the street:

They will prioritize protecting the man's ego and feelings more than protecting themselves from harm or validating their own needs of safety and satisfaction in a relationship. As a result, if there is ever a discrepancy between a man's desires and demands, and a woman's safety and needs, it is the former that almost always takes precedence. Why? Because in our mindset of performing femininity, we learn that "righteous women" disappear themselves from existence and trivialize their own needs to fully center their husband (or potential husband)—even if his behavior makes her feel unsafe, unseen, and unloved.

The long-term side effect of this type of people-pleasing and performative womanhood is that it leaves women with emotional wounding that mirrors survivors of sexual trauma. This is the case even when a woman's only intimate experience with a man is in the context of marriage.

Due to the detrimental effects of this emotional trauma on the psyche of Muslim women in particular, in later chapters in this section, I discuss how this type of female erasure can sometimes feel like community-wide "body auctions" and "sex-trafficking" under the guise of Islamic marriage. While I acknowledge that these analogies might be difficult or triggering to read, it's helpful to remember how much *more* difficult they are to experience for the emotionally traumatized woman living with sexual trauma symptoms every day. This is especially the case when she realizes in retrospect that she was valued most for her emptiness and blankness, not for any unique personality traits or cherished wholeness within herself.

In fact, in the more than forty-five years I've lived as a female soul in this world, nearly everything I've learned— consciously and unconsciously, and directly and indirectly— about what femininity means for the "good girl" could be summarized into a single sentence: *The most highly valued, truly "feminine woman" shows up in the world in two distinct ways: as an empty vessel and a blank slate.*

She's an empty vessel in that her mind, body, and existence are to be filled up by the person she is in servitude to at the time. In childhood this is generally her father and mother, and in adulthood this is generally her husband and children (but mostly her husband).

In fulfilling these roles of servitude, she is a blank slate in that her mind, body, and existence have no unique defining traits except in what someone else (typically her "boss") carves into them. This customized carving by "the real person" (or superior person) in her life thus gives her meaning and direction, precisely through having no meaning or direction of her own.

In this way, her emptiness and blankness are what make her "feminine," and her humble and non-resistant acceptance of her non-personage is what makes her "good."

21

Pretty Packaging at the Lowest Cost

When Nathan pursued me at the skating rink, he didn't see *me*. He saw only an object of desire that he wanted and felt entitled to. He couldn't care less about the damaging effect that his drunken speech and behavior were having on me. I doubt he even processed that he was having an effect on me at all—or that in that moment, I had feelings, thoughts, and fears of my own. Till today, the lesson that this experience has taught me about the wounded masculine stays with me: *They don't see us. They see only what they want from us.*

Additionally, on the flipside as it relates to women living in the wounded feminine, this is the unfortunate truth for us: *We don't see ourselves. We see only what men want from us.*

This is precisely why in the world of performative masculinity and femininity, a woman's emptiness and blankness are not only incredibly appealing and desirable but are also the very definition of femininity and being a "good woman." In the manmade world of feminine goodness that is rooted in female emptiness and blankness, the only thing that distinguishes one empty vessel and blank slate from another is how attractive (or unattractive) the external packaging is on the empty box or slate.

In the context of marriage, this means that women are effectively DIY (do-it-yourself) "empty packages of pleasure." These empty packages are then customized and filled only to the tastes of the men who custom-order them and have them delivered on demand. Here, the prettier and emptier the box—and the less amount of stuff (i.e., "baggage") inside—the more valuable the delivery.

And the cheaper the better.

Thus, even when Allah grants women certain rights, in the manmade world of feminine goodness, "good women" won't even *want* these divine gifts. Moreover, when women who are addicted to performing femininity pretend not to care about a single thing in the world except pleasing their husbands, it gives men the false impression that this type of trivializing of women's Islamic rights and dismissing the divine mercies available to them is something to be expected (or even demanded) of all "good women." Consequently, so many Muslim women seeking marriage are socially pressured (by men *and* women) into effectively auctioning off their bodies and souls to the lowest bidder.

In this type of romantic pursuit—which I think of as "the good-girl culture's guide to halaal love"—the widespread social tendency of women agreeing to marriage sans their rights is more akin to a type of socially and religiously accepted sex-trafficking scheme than the divinely blessed soul companionship of marriage that Allah describes in the Qur'an.

Although this might sound like a harsh description of something that is halaal, I intentionally use this language to highlight how far gone these modern-day practices are from a truly Islamic marriage itself. I also use this language to highlight the long-term emotional and psychological damage on a woman's psyche who has been shamed and guilted into the intimate company and authority of man in a way that effectively sidesteps the Qur'anic injunction that forbids compelling women into marriage against their will:

يَٰٓأَيُّهَا ٱلَّذِينَ ءَامَنُواْ لَا يَحِلُّ لَكُمۡ أَن تَرِثُواْ ٱلنِّسَآءَ كَرۡهٗاۖ وَلَا

تَعۡضُلُوهُنَّ لِتَذۡهَبُواْ بِبَعۡضِ مَآ ءَاتَيۡتُمُوهُنَّ إِلَّآ أَن يَأۡتِينَ بِفَٰحِشَةٖ

مُّبَيِّنَةٖۚ وَعَاشِرُوهُنَّ بِٱلۡمَعۡرُوفِۚ فَإِن كَرِهۡتُمُوهُنَّ فَعَسَىٰٓ أَن

تَكۡرَهُواْ شَيۡـًٔا وَيَجۡعَلَ ٱللَّهُ فِيهِ خَيۡرٗا كَثِيرٗا ﴿١٩﴾

"O you who have believed, it is not lawful for you to inherit women by compulsion. And do not make difficulties for them in order to take [back] part of what you gave them unless they commit a clear immorality. And live with them in kindness. For if you dislike them - perhaps you dislike a thing and Allah makes therein much good."
—*An-Nisaa* (4:19)

In Allah's description of the blessed union of marriage, both men and women benefit from it and please each other. In the "auction yourself off to the lowest bidder" version of this union, by design, it is primarily (or exclusively) men who derive benefit and pleasure from the relationship—except for the financial compensation (if any or much at all) that a woman is paid in exchange for giving up nearly every meaningful part of her life and soul in exchange for the mere *hope* for a man's love and affection.

22

Women's Fairytales and Unrealistic Expectations?

Ironically (though not surprisingly), in circles of performing femininity, even the very love and affection from a man that a woman was promised in exchange for all of her self-erasure and pious self-sacrifice is denied and withheld from her. Here is how this denial and refusal manifests in many women's lives:

Years after she is exhausted from all the self-abandonment and pious self-sacrifice in her marriage, she is told this painful truth, which she (allegedly) was supposed to know all along: Enjoying the intimacy of emotional connection and loving affection from your husband is merely a "fairy tale" that women bring into marriage, and it is just more evidence of the "unrealistic expectations" so many women have in their pursuit of love. Yet this masculine love and affection was precisely what she was seeking when she gave up so much before and after marriage.

This is the moment that many women feel deep down that they have been (to use the language of the late Malcolm X, may Allah have mercy on him) "hoodwinked and bamboozled" into marriage. In other words, this is when a woman often feels in the depths of her soul that she has been effectively "used" for a higher purpose that did not include her own wellness, satisfaction, or life fulfillment.

Yet, during the earliest stages of this effective sex-trafficking under the guise of agreeing to a halaal romantic relationship, the women performing femininity were eager to, as far as possible, show up in the best "feminine package" during the bidding process.

At its best, this feminine package is generally a physically attractive virgin woman who comes with two traits that are in the highest demand: the lowest possible *mahr* (dowry or marriage gift) and the lowest possible standards. If she wants to make herself even more marketable as an empty "feminine package" (especially if she's divorced or no longer a virgin), she can show eagerness in giving up rights to sufficient (or any) financial provision from her husband.

Or if the man prides himself in being a full provider, she can show eagerness in giving up any desire or interest in hobbies or roles outside those of wife and mother exclusively. This is especially the case if any of these pursuits would earn her any personal wealth outside full and complete financial dependency on her husband.

Thus, any woman who goes over and beyond to show up with one or more of these levels of emptiness and blankness is held up as a remarkable example of female righteousness that other women should follow. And in the beginning, this self-erasure is viewed as the ticket to the fairytale of "happily ever after" itself.

RE-CAP

Reason 3

Why Performing Femininity Never Works in Love

Performing femininity asks women to show up empty while true love asks women to show up full.

Compassionate Accountability Prompts
for Embodying Femininity

1. In one part of this section, I discuss my observation that women are often asked to show up as "empty vessels and blank slates"? **Do you agree with this observation?** Why or why not? If not, what do you think is a more honest, balanced observation of what is happening with women today?

2. Reflect honestly on how women are often pressured into lowering their standards and giving up their rights until they are left feeling used and mistreated. **What can we as women do to take better accountability for the choices we ourselves make?**

3. In your own life as a woman, **do you feel that you've ever had to show up as "less than" in order to make someone else feel "more"?** If so, how so? Why do you think you felt (or still feel) inclined to do this, instead of resisting the urge to erase parts of

yourself? Or is there a part of you that feels that showing up as "less than" is easier or more preferable in life? If so, why do you think you feel this way?

4. **Take in a deep breath and exhale slowly until you are in a space of mental calm.** If you like, place a hand on your chest until you can feel your heartbeat. Then answer these questions from this place of genuine self-honesty, even if the answers feel unrealistic, and even if they uncover unpleasant or dark feelings inside you:

   ✓ **What do you truly wish you could have in your marriage (current or potential)?** What traits do you truly wish you could have in a husband? What traits do you truly wish you could have in *yourself* as a wife?

   ✓ **When you think of a "loving marriage," what thoughts and feelings come up?** When you think of an "Islamic marriage," what thoughts and feelings come up? Are the thoughts and feelings different? If so, are there any potential overlaps? Or are the thoughts and feelings contradictory in any way?

   ✓ **If so, why do you think that a loving marriage and an Islamic marriage feel like two completely different things?**

Remember: Be gentle and compassionate with yourself as you explore any unpleasant (or "bad") thoughts and feelings. It's okay to feel and think "wrong" things. This is part of being human. So no, there's nothing inherently wrong with you. You just have some tender wounds that need love and healing.

REASON FOUR
Healthy Love Nurtures Living a Full Life, Performing for Love Extinguishes It

———————————————————

"One of the most heartbreaking things to watch is a woman auditioning for a role she (supposedly) already has—being loved and chosen by her husband."
—from the journal of Umm Zakiyyah

"Healthy love isn't a game. You don't have to 'work' to be loved. You are innately lovable and worthy, just by being you."
—Sheleana Aiyana, *Becoming the One*

23

The High Value Woman of Non-Existence

"If you were truly a righteous woman," a man told me once, "then you wouldn't even have *thoughts* that disagree with your husband, even if you submit to his decision in the end."

In another incident, a well-respected imam told me: If a woman puts in her marriage contract that she has the right to follow the Islamic fiqh opinion that she believes is most correct in front of Allah, then she is asking her husband to give up his entire role as a man—because (allegedly) the man having the final say about how a woman treats her own soul is the entire purpose of *qawwaamah* (men's divinely assigned role of protection and provision for women) in marriage. However, this imam's "Islamic perspective" of manhood doesn't exist in the Islamic faith at all.

In these Last Days, wherein women are most valued for their non-personage; femininity and piety are not determined by our Creator, His Scripture, or divine truth—or even by the woman's authentic femininity or actual piety itself. Rather her femininity and piety are determined by the random desires and demands of men, and by the standards upheld by women deeply invested in the performative womanhood at the heart of "good girl" culture.

Unfortunately, in far too many religious circles, the terms *God, Scripture,* and *divine truth* are viewed as synonymous with some varying levels of meeting the desires and demands of men and "good girl" culture. This is the case even when these men and cultures are not fully committed to God, moral decency, or a healthy spiritual life.

When I speak of the highly valued "non-personage" of women, I mean that the more distant a woman is from showing up as a full human being with a unique soul and mind—and from showing up with unique needs and desires that are all her own—the more of a "real woman" she is viewed to be. This results in "good women" striving every day to become smaller and smaller (and thus shrink themselves more and more) so they can become more and more highly valued in the eyes of men. This is one of the most harmful manifestations of performing femininity.

24

What Exactly Did "Good Girls" Have to Begin With?

When this sort of emotional and spiritual suffocation of the female soul occurs in Muslim circles, it is often defended by pointing to the high reward women will get for their sincere sacrifices when giving up so much "for the sake of Allah."

If we ignore for a moment that all people—women *and* men—earn high reward for any sincere sacrifice made for the pleasure of Allah, we are still left with this unique conundrum when it comes to women specifically:

Sacrificing something or giving up something implies that there was something there to sacrifice or give up in the first place. Yet in the case of women, specifically those conditioned or pressured into performing femininity in the religious context, they often weren't allowed the opportunity to even obtain that "something" in the first place—at least not without paying the hefty price of being shamed and slandered for wanting a single thing for themselves.

Whether it is her own wealth and personal resources, or it is her life goals, hobbies, or even her personage itself, a woman is often guilted away from seeking or prioritizing any of these "selfish" or "frivolous" things in the first place. This is because in environments of performing femininity, each of these is so very often portrayed as off limits to "good women," though this warning is often an implicit, unspoken rule.

In fact, when women are being conditioned or pressured into performing femininity, they are often taught that a truly righteous woman wouldn't even *desire* wealth, personal resources, or life goals of her own, especially if any of these will (allegedly) take her attention away from her divinely assigned duties of being a wife and mother. In this way, women who perform femininity are not allowed to exist in any capacity that even *suggests* an existence outside of full servitude to her husband and family.

25

The Highly Valued Submissive Providers

In environments of performing femininity, there are two key exceptions to the general rule of a woman's non-existence via having no worldly wealth, personal interests, or individual resources for herself, the first of which I discuss here and the second of which I discuss in the following chapter:

Firstly, when a man is afflicted with poverty mindset or is living in the wounded masculine, he will often *encourage* a woman to have her own wealth, hobbies, and resources. This is so that he can use her for his own personal gain. This is a man who actively seeks to exploit a woman's wealth, labor, or valuable resources for an ulterior motive that has nothing at all to do with genuinely supporting her life goals or being a compassionate partner to her.

A man afflicted with poverty mindset or who is living in the wounded masculine might also view a woman's perceived "independence" as a means of sidestepping the fulfillment of his divinely assigned responsibilities. In other words, this man has no genuine desire to be the woman's provider or protector. But as he pursues her for marriage, he pretends to care about all the things she loves and has accomplished. This is because deep down he views her intelligence, talent, and financial independence as a "free ride" opportunity that offers him endless female affection and halaal sex with little to no manly responsibilities attached.

These are men who are best known in mental health circles for their expert level of "love bombing." So, they show up wearing the mask of emotional intelligence, of having deep empathy for women, and of being fully supportive of women's intelligence and talents. However, deep down, they have *less* respect for a woman's personhood than the full provider seeking the empty package and blank slate version of a woman. This is because at least in the case of the latter, he fully recognizes and embraces a fundamental aspect of manhood as defined by Allah, that of providing full financial provision for his wife and family.

This type of love bombing as a means to mask their misogyny is common in Muslim men actively seeking polygyny yet have no desire or motivation to provide for a subsequent wife. However, this mindset also exists in poverty-mindset men seeking monogamy. The women who marry these men often find themselves increasingly pressured, guilted, or seduced into becoming what the social media world calls a "submissive provider."

A submissive provider is a woman who comes with all the stereotypical traits associated with femininity, the most important being full and total submission to her husband's leadership in the home, while also paying her own way (literally) to be in this position. As a result, the woman is expected or required to pay some, most, or all of the living expenses in the home. She might even be paying the man himself in exchange for him staying in a relationship with her.

As one man living this life described it to me, "But the emotional provision I provide for her is more important than any financial provision." Then he said in all seriousness,

"Even if I *could* provide for her, the support I offer her in my presence alone while supporting her in building her wealth and business would make her owe *me* money each month, not the other way around."

Meanwhile, his wife (whom I also knew personally) was each day supporting him and strategizing on how he could build his own wealth and business. As I listened, I realized that he genuinely felt that due to her gender alone, his wife's presence, support, and sacrifices counted for nothing in the relationship because, apparently, it was her God-given job to serve and service *him* without any compensation or tangible value attached to anything she did.

26

Wow Him with Your Talents, Then Throw It All Away

Secondly, in cultures and environments of performing femininity where women are allowed or encouraged to pursue worldly opportunities or to gain worldly wealth, there is often this unspoken rule:

Women should pursue things like personal hobbies, educational degrees, and financial wealth only for the purpose of setting up an attractive scenario wherein they first prove their "high value" through the acquisition of these things. Then once a man offers his full commitment to her in marriage, the woman proves her *true* worth by eagerly throwing it all away (without looking back) in exchange for being chosen.

Even if we ourselves as women accept the widespread culture of using our worldly resources and achievements only for the purposes of beautifying our external package of femininity or of proving ourselves to be "high value" women, there is this additional contradiction in what we've been taught about female piety:

While giving up *part* of your wealth for a good cause is certainly praised in our faith and while sacrificing *some* of what you thought your life would be, is normal (and often inevitable) after getting married, there is no scenario in life or faith in which giving up *any* part of your full humanity is necessary, healthy, or ever required or encouraged by God. (And by full humanity, I mean, your own unique thoughts, feelings, desires, and needs, especially those that are fundamentally emotional or spiritual).

So, why then is this "sacrifice of life" praised in women and often demanded of them in the name of piety and femininity? Or are we, in the name of piety and female goodness, unknowingly rushing headlong into cultivating a self-destructive social and religious environment that was at the root of the pre-Islamic Arab pagan culture of burying female souls alive?

27

If I Make Myself Small, Will You Love Me "Big"?

"No matter how small I shrank myself, I was never small enough."
—from the journal of Umm Zakiyyah

Unfortunately, in these Last Days, it has reached the point where so many women of faith feel pressured into burying their deepest thoughts, feelings, desires and needs— including their most intimate *sexual* desires and needs in the context of marriage—lest they offend, annoy, or inconvenience their husbands. And far too many more feel ashamed that they have any of these unique sexual desires and needs in the first place, so they suppress their sensual inclinations out of fear of appearing immodest in front of their own husbands.

However, the unfortunate truth is, on an emotional level, so many of us as women learned the foundations of this level of self-abandonment in early childhood. For these women, it was during their earliest lessons in goodness and piety that they were taught (directly or indirectly) that a "good girl" doesn't have thoughts, feelings, desires, or needs that could offend or inconvenience *anyone*, most especially not the ones who are more powerful, more important, or more superior than her.

Consequently, so many young girls learn that a "good girl" keeps quiet about her own needs and desires and instead does what she is told (or expected) with regards to fulfilling other people's needs and desires. Thus, any unique thoughts and feelings that a girl does inevitably have should be dedicated to *anticipating* how someone else's needs and desires should be met.

In this way, she is conditioned from childhood to understand that her unique humanity exists only as a means to think of clever ways to make herself smaller, to make others feel bigger, or to more effectively disappear herself from existence. This, so that the lives of her "bosses" become more radiant, fulfilling, successful, and significant.

28

The Step-by-Step Revival of Burying Females Alive

With regards to how this "make women small" ideology manifests in social-religious settings, we can merely look at Islamic history, or pre-Islamic history, to be more precise. In the mindset that views women's non-existence as the most valuable personhood for women, the men and women who participate in (or encourage) this brand of performing femininity that is rooted in female self-erasure are complicit in a modern-day version of burying females alive, even if they have the best intentions at heart.

Here, I am not speaking of the burying of girls alive in the physical sense (though this most certainly happens in some pseudo-religious cultures today). Rather, I am speaking of burying girls alive in the emotional, psychological, and spiritual sense. This is because even in cultures that have historically buried girls alive physically (such as in pre-Islamic pagan Arabia), these abominable practices almost always began by first creating a deep-seated, transgenerational cultural mindset wherein girls were buried alive emotionally, psychologically, and spiritually. Only after this figurative burying of the female soul was solidified in the hearts and minds of the wider society (amongst men and women), the "logical next step" in female erasure was taken: to *also* bury females alive physically.

In other words, from both the lens of human psychology and the lens of socio-political history, females had to first become non-persons (or inherently "less than" persons) in the metaphysical realm before the human mind could become content (let alone emboldened) in relegating them to non-persons (or "less than" persons) in the physical realm.

Even from a neurobiology perspective, the fact of the matter is that human nature (also known in spiritual terms as the divinely gifted *fitrah*) does not allow you to bury someone alive in reality unless you've first buried them alive in your own heart, mind, and soul. In this way, you consciously and unconsciously strip from this person any significant emotional, mental, or spiritual existence, all of which form the very essence and definition of human life.

However, because humans, especially those in positions of leadership and social influence don't like to think of themselves as inciting evil or perpetuating harm of any kind, the effects of the actual harm against any group in society goes relatively unabated and unchallenged for years, or even for generations. In this environment, nearly all evidence to the contrary is viewed as a bizarre anomaly rather than the pervasive, insidious social disease that it actually is.

In his journal publication, "Selective Activation and Disengagement of Moral Control," the late psychologist and former professor at Stanford University, Albert Bandura, discusses this phenomenon, especially with regards to the trivialization of widespread harm in a society by authority figures when issues of major social harm are brought to their attention:

"Authorities usually invite and support detrimental conduct in insidious ways that minimize personal responsibility for what is happening. Moreover, the intended purpose of sanctioned destructiveness is usually disguised so that neither issuers nor perpetrators regard their actions as censurable. When reprehensible practices are publicized, they are officially dismissed as only isolated incidents arising through misunderstanding of what had, in fact, been authorized. Efforts are made to limit any blame to subordinates, who are portrayed as misguided or overzealous. Investigators who go searching for 'smoking guns' display naivete about the surreptitious manner in which culpable behavior is sanctioned and executed. Generally, one finds mazy [i.e., maze-like complexity and confusion] devices of non-responsibility rather than smoking guns" (1990) [brackets mine].

In other words, in the history of human experience, widespread harm first begins on a hidden and ostensibly innocent level of complexity before it becomes a full-blown problem. However, due to the inherent human motivation to avoid appearing as anything but good and sincere, most people—especially those in authority—do not admit any blame or responsibility for what is happening right in front of them and often at their own hands (even if unintentionally). So, they go through their entire lives, often while in a position of power and influence that grants them the ability to remove (or at least significantly reduce) widespread harm, without ever admitting that any significant harm exists at all, or that they have (or have had) any role in it.

To use the language of the Qur'an, these are people who assign spiritual goodness and purity to themselves while doing little to nothing to ensure actual spiritual goodness in themselves or in the society in which they live. Meanwhile, the universal truth of human goodness is this: People who are genuinely sincere, good people are too busy trying to do *actual* good—while openly admitting to their own personal struggles and human failings—to concern themselves with elusive labels of human goodness, which ultimately, only God could know with any level of certainty in any case.

For this reason (and many others), in the Qur'an, Allah cautions all people (male and female, scholar and worshipper, and leader and follower):

$$فَلَا تُزَكُّوٓا۟ أَنفُسَكُمْ ۖ هُوَ أَعْلَمُ بِمَنِ ٱتَّقَىٰٓ ﴿٣٢﴾$$

"...So, ascribe not purity to yourselves. He knows best who fears Allah and keeps his duty to Him."
An-Najm (53:32)

The famous prophetic Companion 'Umar ibn Khattab (may Allah be pleased with him), who himself was promised Paradise and was one of the foremost righteous leaders of the earliest Muslims, admitted to his own pre-existing mentality of disregarding women, which he had to overcome, when he said:

> "In *Jahiliyyah*, we used to have no regard for women whatsoever. But when Islam came and Allah made mention of them, this caused us to realize that they have rights upon us..." (Sahih Bukhari, *Kitaab al-Madhaalim; Baab al-Ghurfa wal-'Ulya*, Hadith 5505).

Yet despite the widespread modern-day practice of disregarding women (often in the name of Islam itself) and thus relegating females to an early death (emotionally, mentally, and spiritually), this is one *"Jahiliyyah* practice" that is almost never spoken about openly or with any significant detail or serious analysis in Muslim communities, let alone amongst our Muslim leaders. The rare exception is when this practice of burying girls alive is portrayed as some bizarre far-gone practice that we of this (apparently) "superior" generation have absolutely no capacity to understand, comprehend, or relate to.

117

29

Understanding Benevolent Misogyny

To any honest soul, the unavoidable truth about burying females alive is this: Any practice of this egregious magnitude couldn't possibly have escalated to the level of murdering young girls as a *praiseworthy* cultural practice, except that it had for many years (and generations) been already made socially acceptable. And this begins with how that society was made to think of the female herself—long before taking her life was even an idea, question, or conceivable possibility.

Therefore, the only logical explanation for this type of reprehensible cultural practice is this: Day after day and moment after moment—often in ostensibly innocent and well-meaning ways—an anti-female ideology was implanted in the minds and psyches of "good" men and women. In this emotionally damaging and spiritually destructive environment, which included the micromanaging and negative critique of nearly every aspect of the female existence (often under the guise of protecting her from some real or imagined significant harm, or inviting her to some real or imagined greater good), a culture of "benevolent misogyny" was born.

In this "benevolent misogyny," *soo'u dhann* (adhering to the worst possible assumption or conclusion about someone or something) was projected onto the life, intentions, and behavior of girls and women. This was especially the case when their speech or actions were ambiguous, questionable, or misaligned with a very narrow idea of female goodness or female "value," even when they were doing nothing ostensibly wrong, immoral, or sinful. In contrast, *husnu dhann* (assigning the best possible assumption or conclusion about someone or something) was applied almost exclusively to boys and men, even when their speech or actions were obviously questionable, harmful, or misaligned with God's definition of morality and goodness. In fact, girls were often assigned blame for boys' immorality.

In this culture of benevolent misogyny, the female existed only to advance the lives of boys and men and to bring honor to her family, culture, or tribe. As a result, any speech or behavior by a girl or woman that suggested individuality—even if she was doing nothing wrong or sinful—was automatically viewed as questionable and suspicious (at best), or as immoral and reprehensible (at worst). If she further said or did anything that incited a man's sexual desire, even if unknowingly and without any wrongdoing or sin, she herself was cautioned against that speech or behavior, or she was outright blamed and slandered as a result.

Rarely (if ever) was the boy or man advised to guard *himself* from sin or cautioned against harming or blaming the girl or woman, no matter what desires her presence, dress, or behavior incited in him. Instead, the inner desires and fears of boys and men were projected onto girls and women and then the mere existence of that "seductive" or "problematic" girl or woman was equated with dishonor.

In good families, in order to avoid any level of "dishonor," girls were conditioned to avoid saying or doing anything that could bring about even unjustified suspicion of wrongdoing or immorality on her part. And since the only purpose of girls' existence was to advance the lives of boys and men and to bring honor to those around her, it was sufficient as a proof of "wrongdoing" for a girl to choose any life or path for herself that was not exclusively in servitude of others. As a result, any evidence of unique thoughts, feelings, desires, and needs on a girl's part was quickly suppressed, shamed, or punished.

In this way (and so many others), long before any young, innocent female body was buried beneath the dirt of the earth, young girls were buried alive emotionally, mentally, and spiritually beneath the figurative dirt of societal shaming, blaming, and guilting—which is precisely how religious communities are burying females alive today.

In the Qur'an, Allah says:

$$\text{وَإِذَا ٱلْمَوْءُۥدَةُ سُئِلَتْ ﴿٨﴾}$$
$$\text{بِأَيِّ ذَنبٍ قُتِلَتْ ﴿٩﴾}$$

"And when the female [who was] buried alive is asked, For what crime she was killed?"
—*At-Takweer* (81:8-9)

RE-CAP

Reason 4

Why Performing Femininity Never Works in Love

Healthy love supports living a full, joyful life while performing-for-love stunts inner fulfillment and extinguishes joy.

Compassionate Accountability Prompts
for Embodying Femininity

1. In one part of this section, I discuss how "so many young girls learn that a 'good girl' keeps quiet about her own needs and desires and instead does what she is told (or expected) with regards to fulfilling other people's needs and desires." **Is this a sentiment you can relate to?** If so, when did you first begin to perceive this, even if you didn't have the words for it at the time? If you can't relate to this sentiment, what were your earliest ideas and feelings about what it meant to be a 'good girl'?

2. **How have your earliest ideas of what it meant to be a 'good girl' influenced how you show up as a woman today?** Or have these ideas significantly changed over time? If so, how so?

3. When you read the chapter entitled "The Step-by-Step Revival of Burying Females Alive," what

thoughts, feelings, or memories came up for you? **Have you yourself observed any non-physical level of female erasure in the environments (or culture) around you?** If so, where and how? Have you yourself experienced any level of this non-physical female erasure in your life? How so?

4. **How would you describe your inner feelings of self-worth today?** Where are you most content with yourself? Where do you find that you could benefit most from self-improvement?

5. **When you think of living a full, joyful life, what does that mean to you?** If you were to begin living a full, joyful life right now, what would that look like? What would change in your life? What would stay the same? **What is one small step you're willing to take right now to make living a full, joyful life a very real possibility for you?** (e.g., Write or speak aloud this affirmation while feeling free to alter it until the wording feels authentic to you: *I am worthy of love and joy in this world, and I choose to believe that my Merciful Rabb wants me to be happy and fulfilled.*)

REASON FIVE
True Love Always Starts Within, Performing Femininity Requires an External Script

"As a believer, nothing you invest your time and energy into should result in a deficit to your life or soul if something doesn't go the way you want or plan. Yes, you will experience hurt, heartbreak, and loss, and there will be many times you'll need to grieve and regroup and then take a completely different path than you expected. This is inevitable in life. But personal and spiritual devastation is not. If the loss of anything or anyone would result in your entire life or soul collapsing in on itself, then you're doing something very, very wrong."
—from the journal of Umm Zakiyyah

"What a beautiful woman. She moved with grace, she was entirely feminine, and yet, she possessed incredible inner strength. She's a survivor."
—Jan Moran, *Scent of Triumph*

30
What Men Like

"I hope you don't plan on getting married again," my friend said, deep concern in her voice. She had called me in a panic after I had announced my then upcoming course and book entitled, *I'm Divorced Now: Heartbreak and Healing.* She wanted to warn me about the heavy price I'd be paying if I decided to go ahead and share my life lessons post-divorce. "Because men don't like that kind of thing," she said, admonition in her tone.

"I'm not even speaking of anyone by name," I said, feeling a mixture of annoyance, confusion, and hurt. "I'm speaking about the lessons *I* myself learned." For the moment, I decided to avoid telling her how it cut deep that she was more worried about what men thought about me than how I myself was doing during this difficult time.

Fortunately, however, after a few minutes of back-and-forth, she asked how I was doing. It was then that I realized that she had indeed called in a spirit of love and deep care for me. The more we spoke, the more it became clear that in her mind, a woman's wellbeing is rooted first and foremost in the positive relationship she enjoys with her husband. Consequently (in my friend's mind), my greatest hope for being emotionally content and spiritually fulfilled was in finding a good man and remarrying one day.

I appreciated her sincere intentions, but I didn't understand why she felt that writing about my life lessons

124

post-divorce meant I couldn't ever again enjoy the soul-companionship of marriage.

"I know women like to think a man should love them for who they are, no matter what they do," she explained. "But that's just not how men are. No man wants to feel like all his business is going to be made public if anything goes wrong."

"But I'm not sharing anybody's private business," I said.

"It doesn't matter," she said. "Just the fact that you're openly writing about being divorced is going to make men feel that way."

I sighed. "Then I guess I won't be getting married again," I said, too exhausted to make sense of what made no sense to me. "If that's really how men are," I added.

After I hung up, I sat reflecting on what my friend had said. I wish I could say that her words didn't bother me in the least. I wish I could say that I dismissed her caution as having more to do with her own mindset than that of men. But the truth is, her words disturbed me to the core.

Was it true that the only type of woman that men liked is the one willing to stay silent, no matter what happened to her, even if she covered a man's faults and sins? Was it true that the only type of woman that men liked is the one committed to suppressing her voice, even when speaking about life *lessons* she learned during her sojourn in this world?

If so, I wondered, *how far are we supposed to take this? And at what cost?*

For me, that was just the beginning of my eventual surrender to my potential *qadar* in this world. Over time, I would see it as a blessed challenge that my Merciful Rabb was gifting me: exchanging a life of performing femininity that suffocated my soul for a life of embodied authentic, femininity that nourished my soul—even if that meant living out the rest of my life in blessed solitude until my body was lowered beneath the ground.

So, I ultimately began to accept that it was healthier for me to stay single until Allah took my soul than to expose myself to a life of self-erasure, emotional suppression, and spiritual unwellness ever again.

But still, I maintained the belief that true men of taqwaa wanted a vibrant, emotionally healthy wife who showed up as her unique, complex self, not a feminine prototype who followed an external script for performative womanhood that told her, "Do this and say this because this is what men want."

31

Is It Really All That Important, Though?

"I've found that I don't care about those things anymore," a friend of mine told me one day, referring to the hobbies and business ventures that had once inspired her in her twenties and thirties, and during the first years of her marriage. "All I focus on these days is cooking and cleaning. And it's a lot more satisfying than you think," she said. "If you do get married again, you might find that you can relax more without all that extra stuff going on."

I was silent, except to thank her for her insight. However, deep inside I knew that for me, so much of that "extra stuff"—like writing books, teaching Qur'an, and supporting other women emotionally and spiritually—*helped* me relax. These weren't "frivolous things" I was doing just for money, fun, or to pass time. They actually meant something to me. They actually meant something to my life. Most importantly, they actually meant something to my soul.

In that moment as I sat processing my friend's well-meaning advice—and the well-meaning advice of so many other women I'd met who were committed to a life of performing femininity, no matter how much they suffered as a result—here's what my heart heard being said to me:

Since men don't care about what's important to you, then you shouldn't care about what's important to you. And your greatest chance at happiness in marriage is accepting that what brings you joy, fulfillment, and soul-nourishment in this world was never really all that important at all.

In other words, I felt as if I were being told: If a man doesn't value it, it's not valuable at all, even if it's valuable to Allah. So, in the end, the value that a man places on something is on a higher level than the value that Allah places on something, specifically as it relates to the value of any work that women do.

As I processed all of this, deep inside, I found this ideology heartbreakingly sad, not to mention a bit tinged with *shirk*, and I refused to subscribe to it.

32

Men Want to Feel Safe with You Too

A few years ago, I was scrolling through Instagram and saw the engagement announcement of an inspirational male life-coach that I follow. Beneath the picture of him and his fiancée, he told the story of how he met his soon-to-be wife and what made him fall in love with her. Amongst other things, he mentioned how he loved her self-confidence, her self-love, and her willingness to speak her mind and even say no to him at times. He said all of this made him feel safe with her and comfortable to be himself in her presence. He also said that the healthy, loving relationship he shared with her inspired him to grow into a better man each day and reach his fullest potential.

He then shared how he was engaged once before, and the moment he realized that his ex-fiancée wasn't "the one" was when he discovered her lack of self-love. He said that he was surprised to discover that she rarely drew boundaries with him, that she almost never said no to him, and that she rarely spoke her mind. As a result, she almost never confided in him about what she *really* thought or felt about something, especially if it required her to openly disagree with him. Instead, she had engaged in constant people-pleasing all the years they'd been together.

Everything came to a head for him after he invited her on the last trip they took together. After they spent time together for those few days, he later discovered that the time of the trip had been really inconvenient for her. However, instead of just telling him no or requesting that they schedule the trip at another time, she dropped everything and went with him. Consequently, she felt bad about everything she had to give up to go on that trip.

The life coach shared that after he realized this type of excessive people-pleasing was how she consistently showed up in life, he knew he could never have a woman like this as a life-partner. He said that having an insecure woman as a wife would in turn make him constantly unsure of himself and their relationship. This is because he could never be sure if his wife was just saying and doing something because she really wanted to or only because she imagined *he* wanted her to.

He also shared how having a people-pleasing woman as an intimate companion would prevent him from becoming the best man he could be. This is because a woman who is willing to make herself small for a man doesn't have the emotional resources to challenge him to become a better man. As a result, he could never reach his highest potential in life, and he simply wasn't willing to sacrifice his success in exchange for a woman who didn't feel comfortable being herself.

When Men Don't Marry the Woman They Want

In an interview with Brandi Harvey, Jason Wilson, author of *Cry Like a Man: Fighting for Freedom from Emotional Incarceration* and mentor to African-American men, said, "Men don't marry who they want to marry because they're not healed" (Vault Empowers YouTube; February 5, 2025).

When Harvey asked him to elaborate, Wilson explained that, depending on the woman they've chosen to marry, many men feel they must be stoic and "strong" all the time.

As a result, they feel like they can never be their full selves because they don't feel emotionally safe enough to be.

Wilson explained how many of these men are often self-aware enough to know that they chose this current woman because she wants only a mask of masculinity (i.e., performative manhood), which is the only way he feels comfortable showing up right then. It is only after he heals his inner wounds and thus feels comfortable being emotionally vulnerable and showing up as his full self that he will marry the woman he *really* wants. This is a woman he will feel comfortable dropping his guard around and letting her see his struggles and insecurities, as well as his strengths.

However, in emotionally unsafe relationships (which men choose because they themselves haven't yet healed), Wilson said that men feel comfortable expressing only stoicism or anger. He explained:

"Typically, we go from zero to a hundred and we express anger 'cause it feels safe for us. [So we can't say] Bae, I'm hurting or I'm sad or I'm depressed. I believe [this inner feeling of unwellness] prevents men from marrying the women they truly desire because we've been conditioned to wear a façade or wear a mask and never show our women [our] Bruce Wayne. They can only see [us as] Batman... It's the men's fear of being exposed for not being stoic 24-7... So I tell men, 'Look it's time to live authentic. If she doesn't appreciate you being a comprehensive man, basically where I'm strong and sensitive, courageous but also compassionate; if she can't take all of you as a human being, then you've been blessed because you know this is the wrong woman.'

...So as men, we have to constantly perform. But when you get married to the right woman, you understand that you are a human being. [In my marriage of 25+ years], when I'm weak, my wife Nicole comforts me, massages my scalp, [and] I can tell her, 'I'm scared.' I'm allowed to

131

feel fear, but I don't succumb to it" (Vault Empowers, ibid).

Men Want Emotional Safety Too

In other words, just as we as women need and desire a relationship where we can show up authentically as our full selves, men need and want the same thing in their intimate relationships. However, this type of relationship that is loving, conscious, and mutually nourishing is only possible if our men feel emotionally safe with us—and if we feel emotionally safe with them.

In this, here's something for us to remember as women, especially if we are still trapped in performing femininity or if we are desperately waiting for a man to *become* emotionally safe for us: Even if a man is the sincerest, most kind-hearted, and most compassionate with us, we won't *feel* emotionally safe with him until we do our own inner work of healing that allows us to feel emotionally safe with ourselves.

Moreover, as a general rule, an emotionally healthy man—i.e., a man who is secure in his masculinity and has the emotional resources and inner compassion to hold space for our wide range of emotions as women—will not desire a woman who isn't emotionally healed and self-confident enough to show up as her full self. He wants to enjoy all of you, not just the prototypical "feminine" parts of you. He wants to enjoy what makes you *you*.

The Feminine Warrior

"Nusaybah [Bint Ka'ab Al Maziniyyah] gained a reputation as the most distinguished woman who took part in the Battle of Uhud... When the battle started, Nusaybah and many other women brought water to thirsty fighters and tended to the wounded soldiers. During the battle, when the Muslims seemed to be victorious, archers disobeyed the Prophet's command and left their battle stations. This action eventually led to their defeat. When it appeared that the Prophet's life was in danger, Nusaybah sprung into action with her sword and bow in hand. She joined a small group that included her husband Ghazzayah bin 'Amr and son Abdullah, who acted as a human shield to protect him from the enemy. Umar bin Al-Khattab said that the Prophet once told him that in the Battle of Uhud, wherever he turned, whether to the right or to the left, he saw Umm 'Umarah (Nusaybah) fighting to defend him."
—Zahirah Lynn Eppard, "Nusaybah bint Ka'ab, The First Woman Warrior"

33

What Does a Feminine Woman Look Like, Truly?

Today, so many Muslim women live by this unconscious rule of female piety, especially while committing fully to performing femininity: *I am willing to do anything and everything to earn Allah's love—so long as it also earns me the love and approval of men. But if my pursuit of Allah's love requires me to do a single thing that risks losing the love and approval of men, then I'd rather jeopardize my good favor with Allah than jeopardize my good favor with men.*

Due to this underlying mindset, it is often other women, not men, who show up to tear down their fellow sisters in faith who have stepped outside the narrow lines of manmade definitions of female piety. As a result, any sincere believing woman who is doing any good deed that is generally unpopular, unknown, or socially unacceptable in circles of false piety is at risk of ridicule, harassment, or slander— privately and publicly. In this hostile, intolerant environment, "unpopular piety" is viewed as impiety itself.

Thus, any private or public criticism of a woman's "unpopular" worship of Allah or "unpopular" practice of Islam is justified through using as a weapon of harm Islam itself. Additionally, criticism of these believing women is justified using worldly claims, such as these women are not sufficiently "feminine." And in this context of performative womanhood, the term *feminine* is defined almost exclusively through the male gaze. But this is not the entire male gaze included in this definition, only the gaze of the droves of men who are performing masculinity or are still living unhealed in the mindset of the collective wounded masculine.

Often, a variation of both religious and worldly justifications is used to tear down a woman who is seeking the pleasure of Allah in ways that are not obviously in alignment with what men desire in a "righteous wife" or in what male-centered women define as a "feminine woman."

This (alleged) lack of righteousness and femininity could look like owning a business, acquiring worldly wealth, having a public social media account, finding contentment post-divorce, or remaining unmarried and dedicating one's life to the memorization of the Qur'an or to the service of the wider community instead of to a husband in marriage. Or it could look like a combination of so many of these things: deciding to own a business, acquire worldly wealth, have a public social media account, memorize the Qur'an, serve the community, *and* be a dedicated wife to a husband in marriage (via marrying for the first time or remarrying after divorce).

But what does a righteous, feminine woman look like truly? Moreover, does a truly feminine woman's strength in one aspect of her life—like Nusaybah bint Ka'ab on the battlefield—cancel out her feminine softness and submissiveness in another, like a sincere, believing woman surrendering to the compassionate, safe leadership of her husband in marriage?

If so, is it then correct to say that women are only feminine when they are soft and submissive to men at *all* times? Or is there room for "stronger" traits in one context and "softer" traits in another?

If no such complexity exists in our definition of femininity or of female piety, then we must face this reality about our own hearts, minds, and souls: We evidently are more concerned with how a random man defines goodness and righteousness in a woman than how our All-Wise, Merciful Creator defines goodness and righteousness in a woman (or man).

RE-CAP

Reason 5

Why Performing Femininity Never Works in Love

●━━━━━━━━━━━━━━━●

True love always starts within, yet performing femininity requires an external, manmade script.

Compassionate Accountability Prompts
for Embodying Femininity

1. In the chapter entitled "What Men Like" I say: *After I hung up, I sat reflecting on what my friend had said. I wish I could say that her words didn't bother me in the least. I wish I could say that I dismissed her caution as having more to do with her own mindset than that of men. But the truth is, her words disturbed me to the core.*

   Have you ever felt internally conflicted about what you were being told about men's needs and wants in comparison to what you genuinely felt you needed and wanted for yourself? If so, how did you navigate this internal conflict? How are you navigating it today? Have you found a "middle ground" that allows you to honor what you believe a man needs while also honoring yourself and what you need? If so, what does that middle ground look like? What does it feel like?

2. **Have you ever given up something simply because you felt pressured to, only to regret it**

later on? If so, what did you give up? How did you feel immediately afterward? What makes you regret this decision today?

3. **Have you ever given up something you initially didn't want to give up but then ultimately felt glad or grateful you gave it up?** If so, what was it? How did you feel immediately afterward? What made you realize this was a good decision for you after all?

4. Look back at the quote entitled "The Feminine Warrior" about the female companion Nusaybah bint Ka'ab (may Allah be pleased with her). **What thoughts about femininity come to your mind when you look at Nusaybah's life?** What thoughts come to your mind about yourself? **Is there a "feminine warrior" who lives inside you?** If so, is she hiding in shame, retreating in self-love, or healthily expressing herself whenever she needs to?

5. Take in a deep breath and slowly exhale. In this relaxed mental space, answer this question: **What are three things you love about yourself, and why?** Spend a few moments thinking about each of these personal traits while expressing gratitude to your Merciful Creator for gifting them to you.

6. When you read the sentence, **"Men want to feel emotionally safe too,"** what thoughts, feelings, or memories come up?

REASON SIX
You Can't Perform Femininity and Embody Femininity At Once

When Women Are Asked to Lead Their Men

"Performative polarity is a harmful coaching practice where women are taught to intentionally 'soften first' to inspire their men to lead with safe grounded presence.

The danger is women are coercing their men to 'act safe and grounded' by submitting first, so their men are not actually leading in safety and grounded presence to begin with.

If a woman 'performs feminine or submissive' for their man, a few things are happening:

1. The woman does not truly feel safe with that man to express freely.

2. The man may be easily triggered, reactive, and defensive, which means he still needs to heal childhood wounds.

3. Your partnership will never develop the sacred union where the man can then hold space for the fullness of your depth because you have been holding back your depth."

—Philip Attar, "What Is Performative Polarity?"

34

True Femininity Is Rooted in Authenticity

"I think what makes a woman feminine is confidence, kindness, and authenticity. It's not just about looks but the way she carries herself and treats others."
—male commenter on "Ask Men" Reddit thread, "What makes a woman feminine to you?"

In truth, femininity is more synonymous with authenticity—emotional, spiritual, and personal—than it is with a static set of traits that we imagine "femininity" to be for every woman in this world.

This means that the closer a woman is to living in alignment with her unique emotional wellness, spiritual excellence, and personal growth, the more aligned she is with what true femininity means for *her*.

In our lived reality as full human beings and unique female souls in this world, there is no "one size fits all" definition of femininity. This is because, by design, divinely gifted authenticity honors every single individual as a unique human soul in this world, whether male or female. Thus, true femininity allows for a wide range of personalities in women—from being soft-spoken to distinctly firm in speech, from being relatively timid to being obviously assertive in personality, from being generally submissive to being unapologetic in drawing firm boundaries in life; and so on.

In other words, true femininity allows women to be fully *alive*—and uniquely themselves—while existing as full, complex, human beings in the shared freedom space of human existence on earth.

35

True Femininity Is Varied and Complex

In so many examples amongst the righteous women of the past, including the Mothers of Believers (the Prophet's wives) and the female Companions of the Prophet (peace be upon him), we find a wide range of what *should* shape our ideals and definitions of "true femininity." However, this would first require us to genuinely care about authentic womanhood in the first place.

For those of us who do care (among women and men), we will find that true, embodied femininity is rooted in a life of taqwaa that nourishes a woman's inner world first and foremost, instead of in a life of performative womanhood that entertains others for external approval, even if this is at the cost of a woman's wellness. And this true, embodied femininity doesn't fit into just one single box of womanhood that so many of us imagine womanhood to be.

Perhaps most significantly, amongst the righteous women of the earliest generation of Muslims, we find a wide range of femininity within *each woman* herself as an individual. As such, when you study the life of any one of these women, you will likely find one trait of femininity manifesting itself in one context and another trait of femininity manifesting itself in another context, depending on the unique circumstances of her life at that time. Moreover, these different traits of femininity that are really just manifestations of personal authenticity—which forms the foundation of true, embodied femininity—are not always "soft" or stereotypically "feminine."

For this reason, any righteous woman who has healthy self-confidence could be authentically soft-spoken or timid at times and could at other times be authentically outspoken or bold. Thus, she can, for example, be generally playful or flirtatious in the company of her husband, but when she senses that her children are in danger, she firmly stands up to anyone who is threatening their safety.

Additionally, a woman could be generally submissive to her husband in marriage while also being an assertive businesswoman in the world. Meanwhile, to those who know her only through her business ventures, she might be described as an "independent woman." Yet to those who know her only as a dedicated wife to her husband, she might be described as a "submissive wife."

Moreover, a woman could be a financially and personally independent woman in reality—whether by deliberate choice or by divinely decreed circumstance—yet be a humble worshipper and sincere servant of Allah. Meanwhile, she can be widely known as a beloved, gentle soul to her female friends and private, close-knit community.

Furthermore, *all* of these perceptions and descriptions of her could be entirely correct and truthful in front of Allah. Therefore, a righteous woman could be single, divorced, or widowed yet show up fully and authentically "feminine" in her life. This is because in the end, true, embodied femininity is merely the lived experience of *any* woman who is living a life of emotional and spiritual wellness, regardless of her relationship status and regardless of whether or not marriage (or men) is part of her life at all.

For this reason, all of the descriptions above (and many more) are manifestations of the lived female experience that embodies true femininity. As such, not a single one of them can be categorized as inauthentic or "wrong." Most significantly, not a single one of them can be accurately described as "unfeminine," impious, or displeasing to our Creator.

Therefore, we can safely make this conclusion about women and femininity: *True femininity is manifested when a woman feels free to be herself while living her life in a way that genuinely nurtures her emotional, mental, and spiritual wellness in this world.*

Are You Performing Femininity or Embodying Femininity?

"When you embody femininity, you are inspired by your own authenticity and thus show up as the best of your true self as a female soul. When you perform femininity, you are inspired by the male gaze and thus are constantly seeking a good 'performance review' based on male approval."
—from the journal of Umm Zakiyyah

36

Auditioning for Love Extinguishes Joy and Authenticity

"I feel like I have to change who I am to have a man in my life," Daniella said. "This hurts my heart." She went on to say:

> "I resent the constant pressure to be a fabulous homemaker. I used to enjoy cooking, but I no longer do, because I resent the pressure… Too often, my ambition is threatening to men. I find this ironic, especially because I don't consider myself to be a threatening person at all. I've been a struggling writer for years now, yet the men I've dated have still managed to feel emasculated whenever I…simply write instead of dedicating every waking hour to adoring them… I have felt as though I am expected to give up on my dreams so that I can support a man's career…or just not have any ambition whatsoever so I don't earn money, I'm powerless, and I'm not intimidating… If a guy I was with really loved me, I wouldn't have to sacrifice my contentment, self-respect, or self-confidence for him. He'd simply accept me for who I am and support me. It saddens me that this has never been the case so far…I am done with this whole notion of 'love'" (Cressman, goodmenproject.com, February 3, 2022).

It's a sentiment that I can unfortunately relate to, feeling the boundless excitement leave my body, even for things I once enjoyed—like cooking, caretaking, and decorating—after being pressured to disconnect from myself and my passions to center *only* self-sacrifice and self-abandonment in exchange for "love."

This is the very essence of performing femininity, and it makes joyful intimate connection with a soul companion impossible. It also extinguishes the genuine motivation you once felt while *looking forward* to pleasing and serving your partner. Once you realize that someone genuinely doesn't want *you* or care about your authentic joy and happiness, it saps all the energy out of you, and there's no possibility for a healthy relationship so long as performative intimacy is preferred over genuine intimacy—and so long as you feel pressured to disappear yourself from existence (or significance) to make someone else feel whole.

37

Performing Femininity vs. Embodying Femininity

Performing femininity asks a woman to audition for a man's love instead of showing up as her authentic self. In discussions about healthy relationships today, we hear a lot about the importance of women leaning into their 'feminine energy' or about the value of 'femininity' in women, especially in the presence of their male partner. But what most women are actually learning is not true femininity, but how to perform femininity well.

Performing femininity is a type of people-pleasing that women are sold as the path to winning a man's heart and living "happily ever after" with him. It is what women are told will make a man fall in love with them and want them as a wife (and then stay married to them).

But performing femininity only serves to disconnect a woman from her deepest self and thus keep her trapped in a relationship that can only survive if she continues to abandon herself and suppress her own deepest desires and needs to center a man's.

Embodying femininity allows a woman to connect with a man from a place of authenticity, and it also invites a man to connect with a woman from a place of authenticity, too. In this space, if a woman is loved and accepted for who she really is—and not because of the "good show" she puts on—she begins to feel joyful, relaxed, and safe in a man's masculine essence. In this space of joy, relaxation, and safety, she naturally connects to what many would call "feminine energy," but not at the expense of herself.

Embodied femininity allows women to be themselves.
Embodied femininity is true femininity, and it is the only authentic, healthy version of femininity that exists. This is because it naturally allows for a wide range of different personalities, hobbies, life goals, and individual temperaments in women.

In other words, embodied femininity allows women to show up exactly as God created them—as individual souls with different interests, goals, and personal paths in life.

38

The Wounded Feminine Performs for the Wounded Masculine

A healthy man is seeking an authentic, meaningful connection with a woman, not an entertaining performance of her "womanhood." For this reason, it is only the unhealed "wounded masculine" that desires a woman who abandons herself and thus denies her own needs and suppresses her own desires to meet his (perceived) needs and desires. But because the wounded masculine is far more common in these Last Days than healthy, secure manhood, there are so many women who readily abandon embodied femininity to perform femininity in a desperate attempt to get and keep a "good man."

However, a truly good man will feel inspired to "level up" to earn the divine gift of a good woman by his side. He would never ask a woman to shrink herself for his pleasure.

Only unhealed, unwell women are content in performative womanhood. Women who perform femininity are generally operating from a "wounded feminine" due to childhood trauma, unhealed emotional wounding, or having internalized society's misogynistic "good girl" conditioning.

Women who embody femininity have standards that they don't lower and boundaries that they don't allow to be crossed. In contrast, women who perform femininity seek love from a place of anxiety, insecurity, and distress—instead of nurturing love from a space of calmness, self-love, and confidence.

For this reason, women who embody femininity don't lose themselves in marriage. They merely find a deeper, more authentic version of themselves during every stage of their relationship journey. In this space of joy, relaxation, and safety, a woman living in embodied femininity naturally connects to what many would call "feminine energy," but not at the expense of her own wellbeing, personal fulfillment, and emotional nourishment.

RE-CAP

Reason 6
Why Performing Femininity Never Works in Love

You cannot perform femininity and embody femininity at the same time.

Compassionate Accountability Prompts
for Embodying Femininity

1. Think honestly about your own life in comparison to what you read in this section about embodying femininity vs. performing femininity. **How would you say you generally show up for yourself and others?** If you're married, how would you say you generally show up for your husband and/or his relatives? **Do you tend to lean more toward performing femininity or toward embodying femininity?** How so? Do you find that you're sometimes embodying femininity and sometimes performing it? What happens inside you (or around you) that alerts you to the difference?

2. If you are unmarried and would like to get married: **Do you find yourself focusing more on what you genuinely want and need in a relationship, or on what you believe men want and need from you?** Is there a middle ground for you where you can prioritize your needs and desires, as well as a man's?

If so, what does that look like for you specifically? **Or perhaps you're not entirely sure what you genuinely want and need at all?** If so, why do you think that is?

3. Take in a deep breath and exhale slowly until you feel a sense of calm mental clarity. Then answer this question honestly: **What are three standards you have (or had) for yourself before getting married (or remarried)?** What is at least one boundary that you will never allow to be crossed, *bi'idhnillaah*? Where do you think this healthy conviction comes from?

4. **Do you find that your own standards and boundaries are not entirely clear to you?** If so, where do you think this uncertainty comes from? If your standards and boundaries are generally clear to you, did any life experience(s) inspire this clarity? If so, what?

5. Look deep within and be honest with yourself. **Which (if any) of these statements below reflect how you feel deep inside (even only slightly)?**

   - ✓ I'm not enough.
   - ✓ I'm too different.
   - ✓ It's not available to me.

Do you find that any of these feelings prevent or discourage you from showing up as your authentic self? Do you find that any of these feelings prevent or discourage you from seeking the love you genuinely want for yourself?

(See the following table for examples):

154

I'm not enough.	I'm too different.	It's not available to me.
For example:	For example:	For example:
"I feel like I'm not enough as I am, so I put on a show of femininity in order to earn someone's love or secure their commitment."	*"Because I'm so different from other women, I can't safely show up as I truly am, so I need to find out what 'good women' do and then do that myself."*	*"I feel like true, lasting love is not available to me, so if I have any chance at a successful relationship, I need to do and say exactly what other people say I must do and say; otherwise, I'll always be alone."*

6. If one or more of the above feelings resonate with you on any level, **how can you strike a balance between being your authentic safe *and* acknowledging the parts of you that genuinely need improvement?**

REASON SEVEN
If You Don't Love You, He Can't Love You

No one is coming to save you.
No one.
So, you have to build a personal bond with your Creator and your
soul that is stronger than any other force in your world.
            —from the journal of Umm Zakiyyah

"If we are unhappy without a relationship, we'll probably be unhappy
with one as well. A relationship doesn't begin our life. A relationship
doesn't become our life. A relationship is a continuation of life."
            —Melody Beattie, *Beyond Codependency*

39
I Knew I Was Ugly

As a Muslim girl navigating the confusing world of American public school, I was riddled with insecurities. Although my mother and father themselves had grown up Christian, by the time I was born, they had accepted Islam and required me and my sisters to cover our hair beginning in kindergarten. That in itself brought with it a slew of challenges, including being called raghead and having my headscarf snatched off almost daily.

On top of that, I had a new "Muslim name" to get used to after having known myself only as Ruby for the first years of my life. While my family and their friends continued to call me Ruby (and still do till today), I was also now being called Baiyinah by teachers and classmates. It was a lot to get used to. Throughout all of us, I never felt like I really belonged, and I felt like I was extremely unattractive.

The first time I remember disliking my appearance is in elementary school. I must have been in the second or third grade when I started avoiding my reflection during school hours, thinking I was ugly. To my young mind, being perceived as ugly by my schoolmates was the most logical explanation for why they constantly mocked me, why they called me raghead each day, and why they took joy in yanking off my head-cover and causing me distress.

By the time I reached high school, I accepted that I'd never be considered pretty by worldly standards, especially since I had to dress so differently from other girls. So, I decided to just focus on my academics and make the most of whatever time I had left before graduating and going to college. As a result, I began to enjoy myself and my own small circle of friends. Meanwhile I remained resigned to the fact that I'd never befriended by the "in-crowd" or asked out on dates by cute boys or anything like that.

However, during my third year of high school, things began to shift for me. As a Muslim, I couldn't participate in most of the fun activities my classmates were into (at least I assumed these activities were "fun" because that's how their "freedom" seemed on the outside looking in), but I did start drawing the attention of boys, being asked out on dates, and even being befriended by some of the popular girls. In retrospect, I'm thinking this shift had a lot to do with not only the natural progression of puberty, but also with my burgeoning self-confidence and self-acceptance, along with my new dress code (which my parents didn't like too much).

Nevertheless, beneath this newfound "belonging" was a distrust in others' acceptance of me and a distrust in my own attractiveness. Whenever my classmates treated me like I belonged or whenever they commented on how cute they thought I was, I felt like I was somewhere I didn't belong but they just hadn't figured it out yet. Over the years I had grown so accustomed to the idea that I was ugly to the people at school that I just accepted it as a fact. Fortunately, I rarely ever *felt* ugly when I was at home alone with myself, but I somehow *knew* I was ugly in the eyes of the world.

This inner "knowing" of unattractiveness created a "me vs. them" identity whenever I was at school. Consequently, each time I was accepted by anyone around me, the feeling I had was akin to being invited to sit in a front-row seat of an amazing movie while never actually being part of the movie itself. At the same time, I felt honored that I was even being invited to *watch*. Some benefits I gained from living in a mental space of front-row seat observation instead of active participation were three:

1) I had the luxury of admiring others, as that involved its own level of inner contentment similar to how watching an exciting movie often does.
2) I was able to live vicariously through other people.
3) I never had to deal with the real-life problems and drama that came along with actually being in the "movie" instead of just watching it.

However, if there's one thing I've learned about life, it is this. There is a divinely decreed universal law of self-awareness and self-accountability that none of us can escape: Whenever you are living in a mental world of your own creation, you are going to get a series of reminders designed to wake you up to your own reality. If you don't take heed the first time (or the first *several* times) that you receive these reminders, then the wake-ups will become ones that are really hard to forget. After that, if you still try to blame someone else for your own painful experiences (which most of us try to do over and over throughout our lives), then you will just have *more* viscerally painful experiences waiting for you the next time around.

Then if you *still* try to run from the lesson and deflect blame, the next lesson is going to crash into you in a way that leaves no doubt as to who is truly responsible for *your* life and how things have worked out (or haven't worked out) for you. One of my first lessons in this universal law came in my last year of high school, and though the experience wasn't catastrophic by any stretch of the imagination, it was life-changing for me as a teenager, as I discuss in the next chapter.

40

She Thought She Was Fat

At sixteen years old and in my self-assigned role (which I didn't realize was self-assigned until years later) of an outsider looking in on the "amazing movie" of high-school life, I admired how amazingly beautiful the girls around me were in comparison to my lackluster appearance. In this, some classmates stood out to me more than others, and one such classmate was a girl I'll call Olivia.

To me, out of all the beautiful girls at school, Olivia's beauty was amongst the most distinguished, and because she had such a kind personality, it was difficult to be envious of her. She was just someone I deeply admired. It also didn't hurt that she was one of the former students of my father (who taught middle school biology in addition to all of his social justice work), and she held my father in the highest regard, as did so many of his former students.

One day as I was watching the "amazing movie" of high school life from my front-row seat, I overheard Olivia say to a friend of hers whose seat was next to mine in class, "I feel like I'm so fat. Do you think I'm fat?"

The question itself took me aback. I couldn't understand how Olivia could possibly think of herself as anything but beautiful because she obviously was. But I said nothing. And anyway, she wasn't talking to me.

"I don't think you're fat," Olivia's friend said. "You're really pretty."

"You think so?"

"Yeah, for sure."

I don't know why this exchange bothered me so much, but it did. I didn't like Olivia talking about herself like that. It irritated me. I wish I could say that my feelings came from a deep place of empathy for Olivia and from anger at the unfairness of a world that would make a girl feel ugly when she obviously was not. But the truth is, my irritation was more selfish than that.

At that time in my life, I wasn't even aware of all the subtle and blatant cruelty that non-skinny girls like Olivia faced that I myself was never tested with back then. All I could see was the attractive physical traits that Olivia had that I did not. Consequently, I was irritated with Olivia for not acknowledging the obvious blessing of her unique attractiveness, which was something many of us around her would've loved for ourselves.

Additionally—and here's something I realized only in retrospect because at the time, this was operating on an unconscious level—I was also irritated with Olivia for disrupting the joyful contentment I felt while watching her star in the "amazing movie" of high school life. In my mental world of "me vs. them," people with more worldly blessings than I had simply did not have similar inner struggles to me, let alone worse. This is like that childish feeling that so many of us can unfortunately relate to even as adults when we see, for example, a rich celebrity stressed out about their personal challenges: *What do they have to be worried about? They have money and fame and everything you could possibly dream of. Give me those problems any day!*

After overhearing that initial exchange between Olivia and her friend, I would hear a similar exchange between Olivia and her other friends. Over and over, Olivia would mention how she thought she was fat and then ask her friends if they too thought she was fat. Then her friend would assure her that she was not but was in fact very pretty. Nevertheless, it was like Olivia didn't believe them because the next day it would happen all over again.

One day, and I have no idea why, but I became really fed up listening to Olivia complain about a problem that (in my mind) she didn't even have. So, when I went to my next class and waited for the teacher to arrive, I started venting to a few other students about Olivia and how she was always saying that she's fat and it irritated me.

"Now, I feel like saying, 'Okay, fine, Olivia! You *are* fat! Goodness!'"

Unbeknown to me, some of Olivia's friends overheard and shared with Olivia what I'd said. Then the next day Olivia confronted me and after expressing her deep hurt, she said to me words I don't think I'll ever forget, "Baiyinah, I would've never expected this from *you*." Then for the rest of the year, she never spoke to me again.

To make matters worse, when Nathan decided to make me the target of his daily sexual harassment and verbal abuse, I sensed that it was this incident with Olivia that made the people who had previously accepted me turn away from me and let me suffer. I sensed that they were convinced that I had likely wronged Nathan like I'd wronged Olivia—and that I was getting nothing less than I deserved.

Deep inside, I agreed with them.

But it still hurt like hell.

Hard Lessons Learned

If there's one thing that sticks with me from the incident with Olivia (and with Nathan), it is this: I matter, my words matter, and how I show up has a direct impact on the people around me. Most significantly, I have the ability to hurt others just like others have the ability to hurt me. In this, it doesn't matter how small or insignificant I *imagine* myself to be. The truth is that since God created me and I'm taking up space in this world (as we all are and very well should be), I can't actually *be* small or insignificant in reality, no matter how insecure I feel inside.

Here's how all of this connects to self-love: When you don't love yourself, you can't *see* yourself; you see only those around you and the effect they are having on you. As a result, you imagine yourself to be less powerful and less significant than you actually are. Amongst other things, this mindset makes you fall into one of two extremes (while sometimes oscillating between both on a given day): You accept mistreatment because you feel you deserve it, or you mistreat others while trivializing the effect that *your* words and actions have on them.

Consequently, when you play back in your mind what happened, you remember more vividly what happened to you or what you witnessed from someone else than what you yourself did as an active participant in that painful reality. It's like something my younger sister said to me during a deep conversation one day: "It is like we have a camera attached to our heads, and when we play back the recording, we wonder why people around us are acting like they are. But we forget that we were just as much a part of that scene as they were, only we were holding the camera."

Today, another lesson I'm embracing from all of this is how self-love is bigger than you. True self-love helps not only you but those around you as well. When you truly love yourself, you have more capacity to be healthily vigilant about how *you* show up because you already know that you matter. Thus, you're not constantly looking to others to show up for you on your behalf.

Also, when you know that you matter, you are naturally more mindful and intentional about making your "powerful presence" count for something, instead of wielding that power in another direction. In performing femininity, that other direction is the helpless victimhood so many of us fall into. This is because the wounded feminine within us makes us blind to the harm *we* are causing with all our hiding and shrinking and restless waiting for someone *else* to see us, to appreciate us, and to treat us right.

Additionally, these experiences have taught me that *lack of* self-love is also bigger than you. That feeling of inner lack harms not only you but those around you as well. Most significantly, as it relates to the topic of this book, this lack of self-love leads to performing for love, which causes its own set of problems, many of which I discuss in the remaining chapters of this section.

Performance, a Dictionary Definition

per·for·mance /pər'fôrməns/ *noun*

1. an act of staging or presenting a play, concert, or other form of entertainment.

> "*Don Giovanni* had its first performance in 1787"

- **informal • British:**
  a display of exaggerated behavior or a process involving a great deal of unnecessary time and effort; a fuss.

  > "he stopped to tie his shoe and seemed to be **making** quite **a performance** of it"

2. the action or process of carrying out or accomplishing an action, task, or function.

> "the continual performance of a single task reduces a man to the level of a machine"

3. an action, task, or operation, seen in terms of how successfully it was performed.

- the capabilities of a machine, vehicle, or product, especially when observed under particular conditions.

—from Oxford Language Dictionaries

41

Why We Perform for Love

Love requires a contentment with oneself, while performance implies discontentment. Yet women perform femininity because deep down, they fear they'll be punished (or rejected) for showing up as themselves if they don't.

At the root of this performance is usually a childhood wound. This wounding taught us that at its root, love is transactional and thus must be earned and could easily be withheld or taken away. So, we perform for love because we were taught that this is what you're supposed to do (especially if you grew up in an environment of "good girl" culture) or because deep down you don't feel worthy or good enough as you are.

In other words, you perform for love because you fear that if the other person saw you as you really are, they wouldn't choose you or want you. So, you speak and behave in ways that you know (or imagine) will impress them, and in hopes that they'll choose you as their "forever love."

Nevertheless, the unfortunate reality is this: Performing and auditioning for love is almost always about a desire for control more than a desire to secure true love. And this desire is almost always motivated by survival, fear, anxiety, or desperation—or by seeking to manipulate another person's perception of you and of the value you bring to a relationship.

However, if you don't show up as yourself in the relationship, it's impossible for your husband to love you. This is because he's never met the real you in the first place.

42

A Bottomless Vessel Cannot Hold Love

If you don't feel good enough as you are, no amount of performing for someone else will change that. This is perhaps the most significant sober reality beneath all of our exhaustive sacrifices on the altar of performative womanhood. In the end, we will never get what we're working so hard for. This is for the simple reason that we're working so hard for something that our performance itself guarantees we will never attain.

In reality, our greatest chance at experiencing true love is to first love ourselves and then calmly and confidently show up as our full true selves, flaws and all. And this level of authenticity never requires us to wear a performer's mask (and it never requires our husband to wear a performer's mask either).

However, if we are going to exhaust ourselves in pursuit of love, then let that love be the healthy self-love necessary to commit to the inner work that brings us to a space of consistent emotional and spiritual wellness in relationship to ourselves, our souls, and our Creator.

But so long as you're performing femininity, you don't have space to give or receive true love. This is because a person who doesn't feel "enough" inside has no inner space or room to let love in, hence my journal reflection I shared in my book, *I Wish Someone Would've Told Me This: Love and Safety for the Female Soul*:

You see, lack of self-love is like having a dark, bottomless empty vessel inside your chest where your heart is supposed to be.

It cannot give love because it has nothing there to give, and it cannot receive love because it has no place to hold it—at least not for any meaningful space of time.

So, it keeps seeking and seeking for something or someone to fill that space, all the while not realizing that this is a space that only you and you alone, with the help of your All-Powerful Creator, can fill.

Then when you seek a partner, they help you nurture and protect what is already there.

This is what it means to invest in healthy, lasting love—and heal our wounds along the way.

When You Embody Femininity, You Live in Holistic Spiritual Femininity

"Embodying femininity is a daily practice and commitment, not a static goal or identity we can claim. Like the spiritual purification of the soul, those who claim it most confidently are often those most distant from possessing it in truth. Because true femininity like true spirituality is rooted in humility, self-honesty, and a spirit of daily self-correction and self-betterment."
—from the journal of Umm Zakiyyah

43

What Does Embodying Femininity Look Like?

One of the things I advise my female clients is this: *Pour so much joy, love, and shukr into yourself that everything you do for your husband (and other loved ones) spills over from this.* Your joy, love, and gratitude in a space of tranquil surrender to your husband then becomes a form of deeply satisfying *sadaqah*, wherein you're spending from the overflow of love and joy that you already have.

Here's what is profound about embodied femininity: On the outside looking in, embodying femininity can often look exactly like performing femininity. This phenomenon is similar to how two people can be doing the same good deed, but their hearts are in two completely different places.

When you embody femininity, the more you choose to give to others, the more you yourself feel fulfilled and nourished. But with performing femininity, the more you choose to give to others, the more depleted and exhausted you feel (and ultimately resentful).

This doesn't mean you'll never feel depleted or exhausted when you embody femininity. It just means that when you do feel this way, you immediately see it as an alert telling you it's time to rest, not push farther. In embodied femininity, your exhaustion is similar to feeling tired at night. Your tiredness or depletion at the end of the evening is simply a sign that it's time to sleep. It's not a sign that you were doing anything wrong while you were awake, and it's certainly not a sign that you should push yourself to stay awake even longer.

Embodying femininity also doesn't mean you'll never have disagreements with your husband or that you'll never have to draw boundaries with him (or other loved ones). In fact, one of the key characteristics of embodying femininity is the ability to disagree without losing yourself and to draw boundaries without feeling restless guilt, shame, or self-doubt.

Yes, you'll feel guilt, shame, and self-doubt at times. However, with embodied femininity, you experience these feelings as signs that it's a time to look inward and assess what's going on in your own emotional or spiritual world. They are not automatically signs that you need to overextend yourself further to please your husband.

Naturally, through this self-assessment you'll sometimes realize that you do indeed need to show up better for your husband, that you do indeed need to apologize for something you said or did (or did not say or do when you should have), or that you do indeed need to make amends after having unintentionally caused a rift in your relationship or having hurt your husband in some way.

However, with embodied femininity, this realization comes from a place of deep sincerity and compassionate accountability, not from a place of toxic shame or blame that puts you in a space of self-loathing, victimhood, or defensiveness. In other words, your self-correction won't come from restless anxiety and frantic people-pleasing, though these feelings can certainly pass through you at times.

Embodying femininity doesn't make you a perfect human, and it's not meant to. Embodied femininity merely makes you a better, more well-rounded, self-honest human being. In embodied femininity, you're consistently showing up in healthy patterns of relating to yourself, to your husband, and to others, even as you (and they) will occasionally fall into unhealthy behaviors at times.

RE-CAP

Review of Essentials

Reason 7

Why Performing Femininity Never Works in Love

If you don't love you, he can't love you.

Compassionate Accountability Prompts
for Embodying Femininity

1. If you struggle with feelings of unattractiveness or feeling un-beautiful, especially in comparison to other women, write or speak this affirmation aloud and then sit in silence and notice how you feel about it (and if you prefer, replace the word *God* with *Allah* if that resonates more deeply with you): *I might not be the most beautiful woman in the world, but I'm the most beautiful woman in my world. This is because, ultimately, the only world I live in is the one God has given me, so I might as well see myself through the lens of gratitude for God's beautiful handiwork in creating me instead of allowing the darker parts of my nafs to make me feel less than, when I'm so much more.*

2. Finish this sentence: ***Some of the most beautiful traits and/or gifts that my Merciful Creator has gifted me are_____.***

3. Finish this sentence: ***Some of the areas that I know I need self-improvement are_____, and that's okay.***

174

4. Finish this sentence: ***One thing I would never want to change about myself is*** _____.

5. Read the following excerpt from my personal journal and then reflect on what it means to you:

That soul-work that you keep beating yourself up about because of all your failings and mistakes? Well, it can only be done imperfectly. That's what it means to be human. And when you feel bad about all your slip-ups, faults, and setbacks? Well, feeling regret is the seed of repentance, and it's how you perfect your imperfections—and beautify your soul.
Nobody gets it <u>all</u> right.
And you know what? That's all right.

6. Now ask yourself honestly, ***How can I be more compassionate with myself about my faults, sins, and challenges?***

7. Read the following affirmations of self-love and confidence, then write or say aloud whichever one(s) resonates with you:

✓ *I am safe. I am loved. Allah is with me.*
✓ *I choose to believe that Allah loves me and is pleased with me.*
✓ *I am enough, and Allah is enough for me.*
✓ *I have enough. I will always have enough. What I have is more than enough.*
✓ *I love myself, and I love my beautiful, imperfect female soul.*

REASON EIGHT
Love Is About Connection,
Performing Is About Entertainment

———————————●———————————●———————————

"If you perform for love, you'll only attract someone who is looking to be entertained."
—Ginger Dean

"I performed for love everywhere. I believed that you needed to earn love by overworking yourself for recognition. I didn't know that the more I presented myself willingly to beg for love, the more I was inviting chaos into my life."
—Elelwani Anita Ravhuhali, *From Seeking To Radiating Love*

44

Clarifying Performing Femininity

"I've been working with a therapist for the past couple of months to unmask and start feeling my feelings," the autistic woman said. Shortly before that, she confessed, "I've recently realized that I've been masking my entire life, and now I don't know who I am." She goes on to explain:

"But it's very difficult because I don't know who I am outside of the personas I create for others. I feel really empty and tired when I'm alone, because I have no one to mask for/to influence what my personality should be. How do I figure out who I am? Does anyone else struggle with this???? I don't really have a safe space to experiment with my identity and try new things that I can't keep private, so I think that plays into it a lot" (reddit.com/r/AutismInWomen, 2023).

I share this woman's story because it offers the perfect segue to understanding performing femininity from another angle due to its strong similarities to what mental health professionals call *masking* in neurodivergent people (female and male). Although performing femininity is not exactly the same as masking, it does share some principle characteristics:

"Masking is a term used to describe the act of concealing one's true identity, behaviours, emotions, or thoughts in order to blend in with societal norms or to avoid negative reactions from others. It's a coping mechanism that is prevalent in conditions such as autism, ADHD, anxiety

177

disorders, and depression, where their natural behaviour or mental health symptoms may not align with societal expectations" (SmartTMS.co.uk, 2022).

Disconnection Is Necessary When Performing

At its core, performing femininity is about unhealthily *disconnecting* from the self and others. If done for long periods of time, this disconnection breeds resentment and unwellness. In contrast, true femininity—like authentic spirituality and the foundations of a healthy, loving relationship—is about authentically *connecting* to the self and others, which nurtures deeply felt trust and gratitude, as well as soul-nourishing joy and holistic wellness.

Furthermore, and perhaps most significantly in the context of marriage, performing femininity, at its root, has less to do with the relationship you have with your husband (or him with you) than with the relationship you have with yourself and your own soul. Similarly, when men perform masculinity instead of embodying it as our *deen* and his own personal authenticity require, a man's "performance" of manhood has less to do with the relationship he has with a woman than with the relationship he has with himself and his own soul.

Another Definition of Performing Femininity

For the sake of this current discussion, I offer this additional succinct definition of *performing femininity* (though its true meaning has layers and complexities beyond the scope of this discussion): *Performing femininity occurs when a woman unhealthily inverses her attention and focus—in life, in spirituality, and in womanhood—until she is living life "outside in" instead of "inside out."*

45

Living Outside-In vs. Inside-Out

Living your life "outside in" means, for example, when you seek happiness for yourself, you're anxiously trying to get someone outside yourself to love and accept you so that you can then feel free to love and accept yourself inside.

Living your life "inside out," means, for example, when you seek happiness for yourself, you first love and accept yourself as you authentically are inside and out—despite any past or present sins or mistakes; and despite any personal faults, flaws, or struggles. Then you seek to enrich this ever-present inner love and self-acceptance by opening your heart to receive and offer love and acceptance to someone else in a healthy, mutually fulfilling relationship.

If you are living your womanhood "inside out" after having sustained any emotional wounds (as nearly all of us have at some point in our lives), you calmly do the inner work, emotionally and spiritually, at every stage of your life. This focus on inner work allows you to first nurture your own emotional and spiritual wellness before you begin to seek happiness from (or with) someone else.

On the other hand, in the context of performing femininity, living life "outside in" is about making your foundational focus either men as a group (i.e., the collective male gaze) or one man specifically (e.g., your husband or potential husband). Keep in mind that, by extension, the latter can include this man's relatives, such as his mother, his father, or any other family. Then only after you process how this man (or the collective male gaze or family) sees you or values you do you interpret (and evaluate) your own inner worthiness or spiritual worth in front of Allah. This externally focused processing of your value and worth can be done consciously or unconsciously. Often, it's a mixture of both.

In the context of femininity (or masculinity), living life inside out, particularly as it relates to *true* femininity (or masculinity), is about focusing first and foremost on your relationship with yourself, with your own soul, and with Allah. Then through these foundational lenses of authenticity, you understand (and evaluate) all other relationships in your life, including the one you have with your husband (or wife)—or the one you hope to have with your potential soul companion in marriage.

46

Being vs. Doing

Love is about being, performance is about doing. In other words, true love is about being fully present with your soul companion while performative femininity (and performing masculinity) is about putting on a show for your partner in hopes of convincing (or manipulating) them into loving you based on your good performance.

What makes true femininity distinctly different from performing femininity is that the former is a state of *being* while the latter is a state of *doing*.

However, this does <u>not</u> mean that embodied femininity requires you to abandon actively doing good deeds in hopes of just passively "being a good person." Rather, **it means you shift your inner world until you consistently do good deeds from a place of inner calm and sincerity** instead of from anxiousness, frustration, mental exhaustion, victimhood, resentment, restlessness, and/or insecurity.

Another layer of this distinction can be understood through the prophetic hadith:

الْأَنَاةُ مِنْ اللَّهِ وَالْعَجَلَةُ مِنْ الشَّيْطَانِ

"*Anaah* (calm forbearance) is from Allah and *'ajalah* (haste or unrest) is from Shaytaan (Satan)." (*Sunan al-Tirmidhī* 2012, *hasan* by Al-Suyuti).

In other words, when you embody femininity as a state of being, you live with the calm inner knowing that your

181

inherent worth is neither increased nor decreased based on the actions, feelings, or thoughts of any other person, even your own husband.

Humbly Hear Feedback without Distress

Here, it's important to note that embodying femininity does *not* mean you dismiss the feelings, feedback, and perspective of your husband. It means that while you sincerely reflect on the perspective and experience of your husband, you understand that ultimately, another human's view of you is *not* the sum total of who you are, your worth, or what you've achieved in this world. Thus, you live in a space of calm forbearance through the inevitable trials and triumphs of a healthy relationship instead of in a space of consistent restlessness and overwhelming anxiousness that make a healthy relationship impossible (though you will naturally *sometimes* feel inner restlessness or anxiousness).

In this healthy space of *anaah*, you live with the calm inner knowing that your inherent worth in front of Allah is not determined by your experiences in marriage (or divorce), or by your relationship status in general. For this reason, it really doesn't matter whether you're married, single, divorced, or widowed—because this worldly label has no bearing whatsoever on your inherent worth as a human being or on your spiritual status in front of Allah.

At the same time, you understand that a healthy soul companionship in marriage does indeed open the door to multiple *increased* blessings and *more* opportunities to nurture your relationship with yourself, with your soul, and with your Creator.

Accepting this balanced reality of life is what it means to embody femininity—in marriage and beyond.

Performative Roles Require Emotional Dysregulation

"In these performative roles of masculinity and femininity, both the man and the woman live in emotional dysregulation, which is heightened when either is upset, scared, or triggered. In this nervous system dysregulation, the woman relies on hyper-emotionality, which unhealthily disconnects her from her mind space; and the man relies on hyper-logic, which unhealthily disconnects him from his heart space. Yet neither the man nor the woman is healthily attuned to each part of his or her nafs, which includes the body, mind, heart, and soul. Meanwhile, this body-mind attunement is the very definition of holistic wellness, and it is the very foundation of emotional regulation and anaah."
—from the journal of Umm Zakiyyah

47

Rational Men and Emotional Women: The Dance of Masculine and Feminine Dysregulation

As mentioned in the quote preceding this chapter, when women are performing femininity and men are performing masculinity, they are both living in emotional dysregulation, which incites the woman to rely on hyper-emotionality and the man to rely on hyper-logic, especially when either is upset or triggered. However, in these respective hyper-emotional and hyper-logic states, both the man and the woman are living with an imbalance in their nervous systems wherein they are unhealthily disconnected from essential parts of their nafs and brain function.

For example, when we are upset or triggered, we as humans naturally experience heightened emotions, and this biological reality is evident in both men and women, specifically in our minds and nervous systems. For this reason, no human being is ever *truly* disconnected from their brain activity or emotional experiences. It's simply not possible. However, we certainly can consciously or unconsciously shut out the *perception* or *acknowledgement* of certain parts of our mental and emotional activity (or reactivity).

Beginning in early childhood, we as humans learn to automatically engage in a proverbial dance of "mentally shutting out" and "mentally letting in" depending on what's happening around us or within us. Over time, what we mentally shut out or let in is based on very specific messages that we internalized during years and years of neuro-programming from our environments regarding what is safe, necessary, or acceptable in our speech and behavior (as opposed to what is unsafe or unacceptable). Consequently, by the time we reach adulthood, we are speaking and behaving on autopilot and in ways we are not fully conscious of, and we remain unaware of our unique patterns of speech and behavior until we make the conscious decision to be honest with ourselves about what is really happening with us. In most cases, this conscious decision does not occur until after we've experienced some form of unpleasant awakening in our lives (or a series of unpleasant awakenings).

For most of us, our initial awakening is quite painful and occurs most viscerally in our intimate romantic relationships, especially the soul companionship of marriage. This is because the intimate garment (and cover) of marriage is where we are forced to see the light and darknesses of our souls through the mirror of someone else. Ironically, the person who ends up showing our darknesses to us is the very person we were trying to impress and win over with all the "light and goodness" of our performative womanhood and manhood.

Yet because our soul companion is more invested in witnessing us being impressed with *their* performance of masculinity or femininity, they can see right through our pretenses and defense mechanisms that are preventing us from giving *them* a "good performance review." In return, we become upset with them as we see *their* pretenses and defense mechanisms, which are preventing them from giving *us* a "good performance review." Meanwhile, neither of us are truly seeing *ourselves*.

185

This is the point in the relationship where we as women tend to become hyper-emotional as we get trapped in frustrating cycles of trying to get our husbands to truly see us and appreciate us or to show us love and affection when we need it most. This is also the point in the relationship where men tend to become hyper-logical as they observe our emotional reactivity with a distant detachedness like a scientist would a subject in an experiment. However, deep inside the man's heart is often a feeling of fear, overwhelm, or frustration because of one of three reasons:

1) He is unable to solve the problem we are presenting to him (even if deep inside, we value his compassionate presence and empathy more than his logical solution). So, beneath the surface of his hyper-rationality is a crippling fear of failure regarding a crucial part of manhood (e.g., having a solution to every problem or being the hero-savior to his woman in distress). And because performing masculinity doesn't allow for a man to feel helpless or ignorant, especially in matters requiring masculine strength, he shifts the focus to the woman's irrationality and emotionality rather than sit with the discomfort of acknowledging anything "unmanly."

2) It hurts him to see us hurt, so he just wants to make the hurting stop; and the only way he knows how to do this is to give us a rational reason why we should stop feeling or thinking a certain way. In embodied masculinity (which is rooted in taqwaa-centered manhood), however, he would be able to comfortably and securely say, "What hurts you hurts me" and then sit in compassionate presence with us until we felt better. This healthy reaction is similar to how Prophet Muhammad (peace be upon him) would often speak

about his deep emotional connection to his beloved daughter Fatimah (may Allah be pleased with her), saying, "What hurts her hurts me."

3) He feels disrespected and unappreciated based on how we are speaking or behaving at the moment. Consequently, he becomes emotionally reactive to us, which is manifested in his hyper-rationality and unloving critique of our speech and behavior. In this, he is failing to see our emotionality as merely a bid for connection and compassion from him—and we are failing to see how our hyper-emotional speech and behavior, especially if they involve insults or harsh criticisms, are making our husband feel distant and defensive.

Performative Roles Lead to Disconnection

On the page that follows this section, I share a visual representation of how embodied femininity and masculinity inspire full-body presence within oneself and also intimate connection between the man and the woman in the relationship itself (See Figure 1). Conscious attunement within oneself is represented in the gray color overlay and with the bodies of both the man and the woman having an obvious body-mind connection.

To contrast this healthy, embodied relationship with the disconnect between the woman and man (and the disconnect between the woman and herself and the man and himself), I share an additional visual representation of how performing femininity and masculinity manifest, which includes nervous system dysregulation and relational disconnection (See Figure 2). In this second graphic of the emotionally dysregulated hyper-emotional woman and the emotionally dysregulated hyper-rational man, you'll notice how there is no body-mind connection with each person's individual body and mind, and how there is also no connection between the woman and the man themselves.

Additionally, you'll notice how the gray color highlights areas of hyper-focus that are activated in the emotionally dysregulated performative relationship (especially during conflict), which is the emotional heart area of the woman and the logical left-brain of the man. The gray lines coming from the emotional heart of the woman and the left brain of the man indicate how each person is pleading for connection and understanding in parallel, disconnected ways that make true connection and intimacy impossible between them.

(Please note that these graphics are <u>not</u> meant as exact scientific diagrams, but merely as visual analogies representing what is happening inside of us whenever we are emotionally dysregulated in a relationship.)

Performative Roles Lead to Body-Mind Disconnect, Emotional Dysregulation and Disconnection

Figure 1: Embodied Femininity and Masculinity Attunement

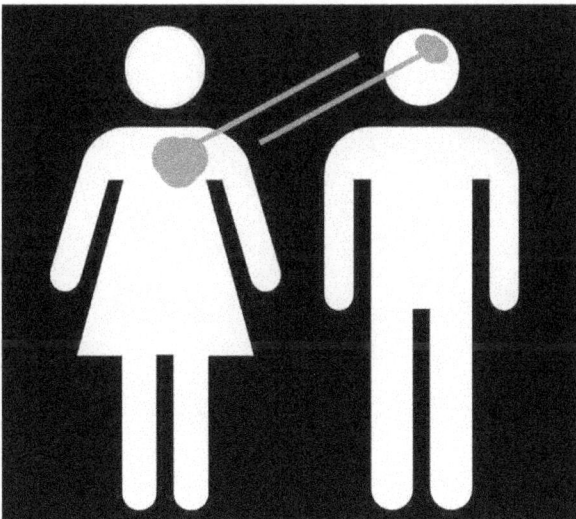

Figure 2: Nervous System Dysregulation and Relational Disconnection in the Hyper-Emotional Woman and the Hyper-Rational Man

When Men Close Their Hearts, the World Suffers

"Whenever a male is not receiving in his heart, the energetic flow between male and female tends to stop. So this male heart has to open to create abundance in the world. If it does not, we are in trouble... Transgenerationally, while masculinity was traditionally defined by what it is not, male hearts have not been encouraged to awaken because it looked like weakness or femininity. So learning to do it is a revolution that combines connectedness with autonomy and self-regulation of the male emotional world.

Searching for the male heart

This is the main goal of the therapeutic menswork I have been involved with for 30 years now. I believe it to be revolutionary because the awakened heart has been the enemy of defensive, controlling dominant masculinity."

—Nick Duffell, "The Impact of Hyper-rationality on Men's Hearts and the Way Out"

48

Avoiding Emotional Dysregulation Is the Sunnah

I know that today many people, especially in the Muslim community, think of terminology like *emotional regulation* or *nervous system dysregulation* as "buzz words" or just popularized fad topics that have little practical relevance to their lives or spiritual practice. I myself thought the same way—until I found myself on the verge of losing my life and faith.

"You have so much cortisol in your system," my doctor told me more than ten years ago, "that your body mirrors a person dying from cancer." She then told me that if I didn't make some serious life changes to reduce my stress, I could drop dead, literally.

This wake-up call sent me on an emotional healing journey that inspired me to make some serious life changes in my personal and spiritual life. Ultimately, I would choose a life of solitude dedicated to regaining my physical, emotional, and spiritual wellness after overworking my nervous system while performing femininity in marriage and motherhood. After years of benefiting from therapeutic resources myself, I became certified in RTT (rapid transformational therapy) and hypnotherapy with a supplementary certificate in trauma and somatics.

During this time of reclaiming my life and faith, I did a deep dive into studying Qur'anic healing, and I began to study the connection between modern-day neuroscience research on nervous system regulation and centuries old prophetic teachings about holistic wellness in our personal and spiritual lives. The parallels I found were quite profound, and many of the most popular prophetic teachings often showed overlaps in what was being only recently widely appreciated and disseminated in the world of mental health and somatics.

For example, we find direct prophetic instructions that clearly indicate the need to avoid nervous system dysregulation, especially when we're angry or upset. We are told to instead take steps to adjust our physiology as a means to regulate and calm our emotions (and thus our nervous systems). In one hadith the Companion Abu Dharr (may Allah be pleased with him) reported:

> "The Messenger of Allah, peace and blessings be upon him, said to us, 'If one of you is angry while he is standing, let him sit down so his anger will leave him; otherwise, let him lie down" (*Sahih Ibn Ḥibbān* 5688, *Sahih* by Al-Arna'ut).

Anyone familiar with modern-day research about shifting one's body positioning and grounding oneself in order to consciously regulate one's breathing and full-body attunement will immediately recognize this nervous-system regulation and beneficial neurobiological advice for what it is.

In her book *How to Do the Work*, Dr. Nicole LePera, who is widely known as "The Holistic Psychologist" says:

> "Emotional regulation is the process of experiencing an emotion, allowing the sensations to pass through the body (rather than trying to distract oneself with, say, drugs or alcohol or an iPhone or food), identifying it ("I am angry right now" or "I am sad"), and breathing through it until

it eventually passes. The practice of emotional regulation enables us to remain centered and calm through the various stresses that life brings and return to a physiological baseline" (2021).

And when a person shifts their body to a position that allows the sensations to pass through the body more seamlessly (such as sitting or lying down), then emotional regulation becomes possible.

In another hadith, we find other direct prophetic instructions about the need to maintain a regulated, calm nervous system, even when one is inclined to rush to the masjid for congregational prayer. In this prophetic hadith, the famous Companion Abu Huraira (may Allah be pleased with him) reported:

> "The Messenger of Allah, peace and blessings be upon him, said, 'When the prayer is established, do not come to it running, but rather come to it walking. You must be calm, for you may pray it if you reach it in time. If you miss anything from it, you may complete it." And the Prophet said, "Verily, when you are deliberately walking to prayer, you are in a state of prayer" (*Ṣaḥīḥ al-Bukhārī* 908, *Ṣaḥīḥ Muslim* 602).

Again, anyone familiar with modern-day research, especially about avoiding unnecessarily activating the body's sympathetic nervous system (e.g., the body's "fight or flight" response, which is activated when running) and instead tapping into the body's parasympathetic nervous system (e.g., the body's calming response that inspires holistic wellness and mental clarity, which is more easily accessed when walking), will recognize this nervous-system regulation and beneficial neurobiological advice for what it is.

There are many more examples like these in the prophetic Sunnah, as well as in the Qur'an itself (e.g., Surah

Al-Baqarah, *ayah* 45 about the people of *khushoo'*), and they all point to the need to stay healthily present with ourselves. This calm, mindful presence allows us to avoid unnecessary states of inner *'ajalah* (haste, restless anxiousness, and unrest) and to instead consistently lean into states of inner *anaah* (calm presence and mental clarity).

49

Independent Women Are Often the Most Compassionate, Feminine, Emotionally Regulated Wives

In February 2024 I hosted a special event titled "Prejudice Bones in Her Body" which I included as part of my Our Beautiful Qur'an Journey (Tadabbur) program. Shortly thereafter, I shared a video clip from the event and posted it on my Instagram and TikTok accounts. I titled this video clip, "Independent women are often the *MOST loving* to their husbands." In this video excerpt from the event, I shared this perspective on femininity in a Muslim marriage: Independent women are often the *most* feminine and pious Muslim wives. I went on to explain:

Men are the providers because Allah assigned them as providers. They're not providers because women are desperately in need of money. Those two things have nothing to do with each other. A woman can be a billionaire and her husband can make $100,000 a year, and he is still responsible for all of their living expenses. His job is the provision because Allah assigned it to him.

Additionally, as a woman, there is no contradiction between me having complete financial independence and also calmly in my "feminine energy" accepting the provision of a man. This is very important for women to understand, especially because so many of us are taught that we need to be "ready-made wives." In this, we're taught that the more helpless we are and the less money we have, the more able we are to be in our feminine energy, and that's simply not true.

In fact, the women who actually are able to be in their feminine energy the *most* and are the most able to fulfill the obligations of the wife are the women who are the most self-sufficient in the world. There is so much research to support this, and more importantly, as it relates to the Muslim experience, there is proof in Islam for this, and we need to understand this.

As a woman, the less you actually "need" a man, the more you can calmly be in your feminine energy and thus be a source of support and compassionate presence for your husband, even when he steps outside of himself. For example, Prophet Muhammad (peace be upon him) spoke about the women of Paradise and included the description of a woman who gets angry with her husband or is mistreated by him, yet she says to him, "Here is my hand in your hand, I will not sleep until you are pleased" (*al-Silsilah al-Saheehah*, 3380; *hasan* by al-Albaani).

If we are performing femininity and thus are in a space of anxious people pleasing and helpless dependency on our husbands, reading this description of a righteous woman can be triggering and actually seem like oppression. However, in this hadith the Prophet (peace be upon him) is not talking about abuse, he is talking about isolated incidents of wrongdoing that are inevitable in any relationship. Sometimes we will wrong our husband, and sometimes he will wrong us.

In these cases, a woman who is in her healthy feminine energy and is not desperately depending on her husband— whether for her identity, for approval, for seeing herself as the best woman in the world (or as the worst woman in the world), or for every means of her practical survival—is the one who has the most access to her inner emotional resources, especially when she herself is upset while her husband is *also* upset. This healthy level of practical and emotional self-sufficiency allows her to show up in the very specific way described in the prophetic hadith.

Healthily independent women generally have their own identity and sense of self-worth that is completely separate from their husbands; and thus don't "need" a relationship for survival. As a result, they aren't as negatively affected by their husband's moments of unkindness as is a woman living in performing femininity, who likely has self-sacrificed to the point of exhaustion. The woman who sees femininity as female helplessness and self-erasure is likely to have little or no emotional resources to offer her husband in his moments of anger and wrongdoing. Instead, she'll likely feel victimized by her husband's unkind behavior and thus need him to comfort *her*. Yet in this moment, he is not in an emotional space to even be present for himself, let alone someone else.

And there's nothing wrong with this. No human being can be healthily and fully present with themselves 24-7, and no human being can show up in compassion and empathy for others every single moment of the day. We all have moments of disconnect from ourselves and neglect or mistreatment of others (though prayerfully not on an extreme or toxic level).

This is where having a healthy, loving embodied relationship is very helpful. In these moments where we forget ourselves and unintentionally neglect or wrong our loved ones, if we are not engaged in performative womanhood or manhood, we can have someone by our side who is a compassionate mirror to us. This is a loving soul companion who when they see us upset or triggered will kindly place their hands in ours and say in all sincerity and compassion, "I'm here for you, and I'm not going anywhere until you are okay."

Are Alpha Males Natural Leaders?

"The best description I ever heard a man give of an 'alpha male' is one that includes traits that many would consider beta. This true alpha male is kind, compassionate, empathetic, and humble—not because he is weak, but because his unique strength and authoritativeness are already clear. This alpha male is a natural leader whose position of leadership is both well-established and not in dispute. Thus, when he exhibits kindness, compassion, and empathy to others; it is his way of 'lowering a wing of humility' to those under his protection and care. He is not doing this because he is beta, but because what the people are experiencing genuinely matters to him, and he wants them to know that he cares. In this context, the terms alpha and beta become relevant only when other men are vying for this position. But it is only the alpha male who is the natural leader and thus does not need to vie for this position at all. However, there are times that he might need to defend his status as leader, particularly when it is challenged by those who have no business leading at all."
—from the journal of Umm Zakiyyah

50

Performative Manhood Fixates on the Alpha Male

Men and women who think the ideal manifestations of womanhood and femininity are female helplessness and excessive dependency on men as opposed to healthy independence and self-love within a woman's own soul also have very specific ideas of what a "real man" is and is not. In this narrow mental space, they often use labels like "alpha male" and "beta male" to distinguish between men they view as strong "real men" as opposed to men they view as weak "simps."

Although there are people who use terms like *alpha male* and *beta male* to merely describe the natural variations in men's personalities and emotional makeups that God has decreed for all humans—or to differentiate "natural leaders" from "natural followers"—there are many men and women whose use of these terms conveys something else entirely. In the case of men and women who see the alpha-male description as almost unilaterally positive and the beta-male description as unilaterally negative, their use of these terms merely reflects the truth of their own unhealed emotional states, which they project onto the world around them. These are people whose wounds tell them that alpha men are "strong" and dominating and beta men are "soft" and overly sensitive.

Muslims who see the world through their wounding more than their *deen* (spiritual way of life) go as far as to project these limited, unhealed perceptions onto our beloved Prophet Muhammad (peace be upon him), his Companions (male and female), and the Mothers of Believers (may Allah be pleased with them). As a result, they boldly claim that the Prophet was an alpha male (as opposed to a "weak" beta male), as (allegedly) also were his closest and the most rightly guided male companions. Similarly, these Muslims boldly claim that the wives of the Prophet, along with the most righteous and highly praised of the female companions, were generally docile, submissive women who quietly and devoutly obeyed their husbands and surrendered fully to male leadership without any resistance, strong opinions, or "backtalk."

However, the reality is that very few (if any) of these celebrated and well-known female companions fit easily into the weak, docile image of a prototypical feminine woman that is most celebrated today in circles of performative womanhood and manhood. Moreover, the Prophet Muhammad (peace be upon him) himself, despite his well-known strength and bravery as a Muslim leader, does not fit easily into the stereotypical image of a hyper-masculine male as it popularly understood today.

In fact, many (if not most) of the personality traits of the Prophet (peace be upon him)—though he is indisputably a natural leader—could arguably fit more easily into the category of the "beta male" than that of the alpha male, as I discuss in the next chapter.

Of Monikers and Men

"If you've been online recently, you may have heard phrases like 'beta' and 'sigma' male tossed around. While these terms may (quite literally) sound like a foreign language…they're actually pretty simple monikers that pop culture sites use to describe various types of men… Alpha males are fearless trailblazers who love to be in control while beta males are kind, gentle souls who prioritize personal connections…"
—Finn Kobler and WikiHow.com, "From Alpha to Omega: A Guide to the 7 Male Personalities"

51

Was the Prophet ﷺ a Beta Male?

Before delving into the question mentioned in the title of this chapter, I'd like to clarify two relevant points as it relates to my discussion of this topic as a Muslim woman:

Firstly, this question is meant as more rhetorical and thought-provoking than as earnestly seeking a definitive answer. This is mainly because, in the Islamic context, whenever discussing terms and labels that do not exist in the language of the Qur'an and Sunnah, no convincing argument can be made that automatically leads to a clear "right" or "wrong" answer. As it relates to the topic of this chapter specifically, the terms *alpha* and *beta* simply do not exist in the Islamic context; and in prophetic history, they never have. Furthermore, even in the current cultural contexts in which these terms actively exist in both secular and religious circles, these terms remain both novel and subjective. They additionally reflect a controversial ideology that began at the very introduction of the term *alpha male*.

For example, in an online article published by *Business Insider*, author Rafi Letzer asserts in the title itself: "There's no such thing as an alpha male." He goes on to explain the origin of this term *alpha male*, saying it was originally meant to describe wolf behavior:

> "David Mech introduced the idea of the alpha to describe behavior observed in captive animals Alphas, he wrote in his 1970 book, *The Wolf: Ecology and Behavior of an*

Endangered Species, win control of their packs in violent fights with other males." (2016).

In another article published by *Scientific American*, the origin of the term *alpha male* is further clarified in the context of debunking this alpha-wolf (and thus alpha-male) concept as a biological and cultural myth, specifically as it relates to "natural" masculinity:

> "The idea that wolf packs are led by a merciless dictator, or alpha wolf, comes from old studies of captive wolves. In the wild, wolf packs are simply families. If you've ever heard the term 'alpha wolf,' you might imagine snapping fangs and fights to the death for dominance. The idea that wolf packs are led by a merciless dictator is pervasive, lending itself to a shorthand for a kind of dominant masculinity. But it turns out that this is a myth, and in recent years wildlife biologists have largely dropped the term 'alpha.' In the wild, researchers have found that most wolf packs are simply families, led by a breeding pair, and bloody duels for supremacy are rare" (February 28, 2023).

In other words, modern-day research itself confirms that the term *alpha* is both relatively new and inherently problematic, as even in its inception, the term *alpha* was meant to describe a merciless, blood-thirsty animalistic "leader." This hyper-masculine male animal gained his alpha status by dominating others and violently taking ownership of "the weak"; and at the end of the bloody fight for dominance, whoever is left standing (or alive) wins. Even if we ignore for a moment that this "natural reality" of masculinity has been proven false in the same biological context from whence it came, the original understanding of the term itself begs the question: *Who in their right mind would think this animalistic mindset in a human being is a* good *thing?*

Is This Really Our Idea of True Manhood?

When understood by its original meaning in the context of masculinity and "real manhood" in humans, it becomes undeniably clear that the term *alpha* is simply one ideological branch of worldviews like Western imperialism and Darwin's "survival of the fittest" to describe human relationships on earth. As such, the celebration of masculine strength as manifested in the "alpha male" is at the root of mindsets that praise (and support) everything from the Zionistic destruction of Palestine to unapologetic misogyny and white supremacy in the Western world.

Consequently, regardless of what our personal (or favored) definition of the term *alpha male* might be, which very well might be much more nuanced and generous than its original animalistic definition, this point remains undeniable: The alpha description of manhood is, by its very nature, subject to a wide range of varying ideas of masculinity that differ from person to person, context to context, and culture to culture. Moreover, it is very rare (though certainly not non-existent) that any hardline "alpha-male" definition conveys anything remotely praiseworthy from the Islamic perspective. Additionally, it is very rare that the alpha-male construct encapsulates the nuances and divinely blessed complexities of taqwaa-centered manhood that is firmly rooted in the prophetic example.

But What About the Beta Male?

Secondly, before I respond to the chapter's question: *"Was the Prophet ﷺ a beta male?"* I'd like to clarify this additional point: I myself (both as Umm Zakiyyah the woman and personality, and as Umm Zakiyyah the author of this book) am not invested in specific labels and terminology. Instead, I am invested in healthy concepts of masculinity and femininity, in getting to "the heart" of an issue, and in our collective and individual self-honesty as men and women. This, in hopes of our collective and personal healing and self-betterment.

Therefore, if any reader dislikes the term *beta male*, I say this: For the purposes of this discussion, feel free to discard this term entirely and mentally replace it with something more palatable—so long as this new term conveys a "non-alpha" concept of manhood as it relates to the alpha-male/wolf version of masculinity defined above. I make this suggestion because in this context, the "beta male" label is less relevant than this salient point: The alpha-male description of Allah's Prophet (peace be upon him) is at best unclear (and thus inherently problematic) and at worst dangerous and destructive (and thus potentially harmful), especially when applied to male-female marital relationships.

Additionally, this alpha-male description of prophetic masculinity simply does not match the *actual* personality of Prophet Muhammad (peace be upon him) in comparison to the personality that so many of us are imagining or projecting onto him, whether with good intentions or for our own selfish motives. This non-alpha description of the Prophet's true nature is evident whether we are looking at how Muhammad Ibn Abdullah (peace be upon him) showed up before the assignment of prophethood or after it. Any honest study of his life reveals that he had a gentle nature and non-dominating personality that followed him all throughout his life.

Can Beta-Male Describe the Prophetic Personality?

If we look at the following list of personality traits that place a man in the category of being a beta male, as published on verywellmind.com, we'll find that many of these describe personality traits that were well-known within the Prophet (peace be upon him) himself:

- Collaborating and cooperating with others to make a decision
- Struggles with saying "no" and [with] being firm with boundaries
- Not competitive
- Friendly and warm
- Comfortable with emotions and intimacy
- Respects leadership
- Loyal
- Does not have a big ego
- Prefers to follow and not lead
- Trustworthy and reliable (2024).

Interestingly, one of the most ostensibly negative traits on this list (i.e., Struggles with saying "no" and being firm with boundaries) was listed as an inner *struggle* of the beta male instead of something that is inherently bad, weak, or blameworthy in the man. Even more interesting, at least from the Muslim perspective, is that it is well-documented that Prophet Muhammad (peace be upon him) himself experienced both of these struggles (i.e., saying no and being firm with boundaries).

Would an Alpha Male Struggle with Saying No?

In the Qur'an, Allah says:

يَٰٓأَيُّهَا ٱلَّذِينَ ءَامَنُواْ لَا تَدْخُلُواْ بُيُوتَ ٱلنَّبِيِّ إِلَّآ أَن يُؤْذَنَ لَكُمْ إِلَىٰ طَعَامٍ غَيْرَ نَٰظِرِينَ إِنَىٰهُ وَلَٰكِنْ إِذَا دُعِيتُمْ فَٱدْخُلُواْ فَإِذَا طَعِمْتُمْ فَٱنتَشِرُواْ وَلَا مُسْتَـْٔنِسِينَ لِحَدِيثٍ إِنَّ ذَٰلِكُمْ كَانَ يُؤْذِى ٱلنَّبِيَّ

فَيَسْتَحْيِۦ مِنكُمْ وَٱللَّهُ لَا يَسْتَحْيِۦ مِنَ ٱلْحَقِّ

"O you who have believed, do not enter the houses of the Prophet except when you are permitted for a meal, without awaiting its readiness. But when you are invited, then enter; and when you have eaten, disperse without seeking to remain for conversation. Indeed, that [behavior] was troubling the Prophet, and he is shy of [dismissing] you. But Allah is not shy of the truth..."
—*Al-Ahzaab* (33:53)

If we look at the occasion of revelation for this ayah, we see that it pertains to the dinner held after the Prophet's marriage to Zainab (may Allah be pleased with her). During this dinner, the people overstayed their welcome and the Prophet (peace be upon him) wanted them to leave, but he was too shy to tell them, which clearly indicates a struggle with saying no and drawing boundaries. The Companion Anas (may Allah be pleased with him) describes part of this incident as follows:

"I saw that Allah's Messenger (ﷺ) served us bread and meat until it was broad day light and the people went away, but some persons who were busy in conversation stayed on in the house after the meal. Allah's Messenger (ﷺ) also went out and I also followed him, and he began to visit the apartments of his wives... He moved on until he entered the apartment, and I also went and wanted to enter (the apartment) along with him, but he threw a curtain between me and him, as (the verses pertaining to seclusion) had been revealed, and people were instructed in what they had been instructed" (Sahih Muslim, 1428b).

In another famous incident, the Prophet (peace be upon him) decided to never again eat honey despite his love for it because he wanted to avoid displeasing his wives. In response, Allah intervened by revealing the first verses of Surah 66 (At-Tahreem) and gently reprimanded him for this decision while also reprimanding the wives involved in making him feel this way. However, the initial decision itself is evidence of the Prophet's gentle personality and how he struggled with boundaries at times due to his sensitivity and shyness, two traits that are generally associated with the beta male. Meanwhile, in popular understandings of masculinity today, an alpha male would never readily give up something he loved just to please a woman, especially if that thing was obviously beneficial for his health as honey obviously is.

In Islam, however, sensitivity and compassion, along with having a kind, generous nature are viewed as essential parts of faith and traits that encapsulate good character. These essential traits of a sincere Muslim include:

1) *rahmah* (mercy), which is the foundation of Islam itself, as described in ayah 107 of Surah 21 (Al-Anbiyaa')
2) *marhamah* (compassion and empathy), which is a trait of the believers, as described in ayah 17 of Surah 90 (Al-Balad)
3) *hayaa'* (shyness and a healthy sense of shame), which is described in a prophetic hadith as a part of *emaan* (true faith)

In fact, a person who struggles with boundaries and saying no in the way that the Prophet (peace be upon him) did during Zainab's wedding dinner is demonstrating a type of *hayaa'* rooted in having a soft, generous heart. In an article titled "Ḥayā': More Than Just Modesty in Islam," Sheikh Mohammad Elshinawy mentions "The ten shades of *ḥayā*'" when he says that in *Madārij al-Sālikīn*, Ibn al-Qayyim subdivided *ḥayā'* into ten categories [including]:

"The *ḥayā'* of generosity; this is like the *ḥayā'* of the Prophet ﷺ from those he invited to Zaynab's wedding dinner. They overstayed their welcome, but he ﷺ was too shy to tell them, so he simply stood and left" (cited via YaqeenInstitute.org; August 5, 2021).

Interestingly, implied in this detailed discussion of *hayaa'* is deep emotional connection to oneself and one's loved ones, which necessitates embodied femininity and masculinity as opposed to performative versions of womanhood and manhood, which necessitate disconnect.

As it relates to taqwaa-centered manhood and embodied masculinity, we can conclude the following about a man struggling with boundaries but then ultimately following through and doing what is necessary: *The struggle is a sign of compassion, and the follow-through is a sign of manhood.*

Healthier Connection Means Healthier Boundaries

"The hardest thing about implementing boundaries is accepting that some people won't like, understand, or agree with yours. Once you grow beyond pleasing others, setting your standards becomes easier. Not being liked by everyone is a small consequence when you consider the overall reward of healthier relationships."
—Nedra Glover Tawwab, *Set Boundaries, Find Peace: A Guide to Reclaiming Yourself*

52

Seven Signs You're Performing for Love

At the heart of performing for love is the motivation to control another person's perception of you and to ensure that they see only what you think they want to see and what will increase your value in their eyes.

Although this type of performative intimacy is often accurately defined as "manipulation" in the technical sense of the term, the underlying negative connotation of this terminology can be misleading, and even unfair, in certain contexts. For example, when it comes to oppressed and underprivileged groups performing for the acceptance of those who systemically harm them, this behavior is more accurately labeled as a tool of survival. This is because the subjugated person is showing up this way only as a means to protect themselves from harm due to their conscious or unconscious awareness that the more powerful person will inflict harm on them for *not* showing up in this way.

Nevertheless, no matter our personal circumstances in life, it always is in our best interest—and is in fact our personal responsibility for the health of our souls—to strive our level best to show up as our authentic selves wherever it is safe, wise, and feasible to do so. While our ability to remain unharmed while remaining authentic will naturally vary from person to person depending on our level of privilege, our individual culture, and our unique personal circumstances, here's something to always keep in mind:

One area that we should be especially vigilant in preserving our authenticity and being sure to show up as our authentic selves as far as possible is in how we show up in pursuit (or preservation) of love and companionship in marriage. This is especially crucial for women, who generally suffer the greatest long-term harm (mentally, emotionally, and physically) when they exchange authenticity for approval, as the act of performing femininity asks us to do.

So, here are seven signs to look for within yourself that alert you to signs that you're performing femininity instead of embodying femininity, often in hopes of earning (and securing) a man's love:

1) You're more invested in what a man thinks about you than in what you think about yourself.
2) You're more focused on how a man feels in your presence than on how you feel in your own presence, and in your own body, mind, and soul.
3) You rarely if ever feel beautiful unless a man has given you a compliment or has shown interest in you.
4) You constantly worry if your needs are "too much" or your standards are too high.
5) You often keep quiet about things that are important to you out of fear of how you'll appear to a man or how you might offend (or intimidate) a man.
6) You often stuff down your feelings or adjust your behavior and speech to fit into what you know (or imagine) a man desires, asks, or requires of you.
7) You're willing to give up your life goals, personal preferences, and deeply meaningful pursuits to make a man happy (or to make a man feel less intimidated by you), even as you know (or fear) deep down that

this sacrifice will be emotionally harmful to you long-term, spiritually difficult as a lifestyle, or consistently agonizing (or suffocating) to your inner self.

But Shouldn't We Want to Please Our Husbands?

"Embodying femininity isn't about never seeking to please a man. It's about showing up as your authentic self and then seeking to connect with your loved ones from this place. When you show up authentically, you will enjoy doing things that bring pleasure to the ones you love, including and most especially your husband.
But when you're constantly showing up from a place of seeking approval outside yourself, you'll likely ultimately exhaust your soul until bringing pleasure to others feels like a costly sacrifice or overwhelming chore. Overtime, this leads to burnout, resentment, and for many women, spiritual crisis.
This is why, in the long run, performing femininity is quite literally harmful to your soul."
—from the journal of Umm Zakiyyah

RE-CAP

Reason 8
Why Performing Femininity Never Works in Love

●──────────────●

Love is about connection. Performing is about entertainment.

Compassionate Accountability Prompts
for Embodying Femininity

1. In the chapter entitled "Being vs. Doing," I mention this prophetic hadith: *"Anaah* (calm forbearance) is from Allah and *'ajalah* (haste or unrest) is from Shaytaan (Satan)." (*Sunan al-Tirmidhī* 2012). Here, it is important to note that just because something is from Shaytaan, like *'ajalah*, doesn't mean that we are bad or sinful if we struggle with it. Nearly all humans face inner restlessness and sometimes have a difficult time finding their inner calm. So, we can understand this hadith in this way: **Being in a space of inner calm rooted in nervous system regulation allows for goodness and healing to take place, while being in a space of inner unrest rooted in nervous system dysregulation opens the door to harm and unwellness.**

   Look deep within and be honest with yourself: **Would you say that you generally show up to life** with a constant sense of *anaah* (inner calm) or with a constant sense of *'ajalah* (inner restlessness) or anxiety? As far as you can recall, what are your earliest memories of showing up to life in this way? Where did you learn this, and why?

2. Look deep within and be honest with yourself: **Do you generally find yourself living "inside out" or "outside in"?** How so?

3. As aforementioned, struggles with *'ajalah* (unrest within the *nafs*) are a natural part of being human, and **this lack of inner calm is at the very core of nervous system dysregulation (or emotional dysregulation).** For those of us living with unhealed emotional wounds (especially if they began in childhood), our challenges with nervous system dysregulation are multiplied. The good news is that the more we allow our nervous system to be a space of *anaah* (inner calm and mental clarity), the more able we are to heal our core emotional wounds. So, healing becomes most possible when our nervous system is most regulated.

   What is one small thing you're willing to commit to each day to inspire *anaah* (inner calm) in your nervous system? (e.g., box breathing, meditation, mindfulness, increasing *khushoo'* in Salaah, praying Witr or Tahajjud in the last third of the night before Fajr, calmly extending your *sujood* for a few extra seconds, etc.). Keep in mind, if you want to heal any underlying emotional wounds or to overcome any personal challenges stemming from earlier trauma, know this: **All healing begins with a calm, regulated nervous system.** So, be sure to prioritize *anaah*, no matter what other healing methods you use.

4. Think of a struggle that you face each day that constantly incites anxiety, shame, or overwhelm in you. Now take in a deep breath and exhale slowly, then **write or speak this loving affirmation of self-compassion three times:** *Just be and let it be.* (Here, we do <u>not</u> mean that we give up on ourselves or our souls. We just mean that we will be loving and compassionate with ourselves as we gently hold ourselves accountable each day).

5. When you read the discussions about *alpha male* vs. *beta male*, and about the character traits of the Prophet (peace be upon him), **what thoughts and feelings came up for you?** Do you have another perspective on this topic that is different from what was discussed here? If so, what is your perspective?

6. In the chapter entitled, "Seven Signs You're Performing for Love," did you recognize yourself in any one or more of the seven signs? If so, which ones? **What is one step toward embodying femininity that you feel safe and comfortable taking right now?** (e.g., *I'll begin journaling about my feelings, boundaries, and life goals so that they become real for me and I no longer shame myself for them*).

REASON NINE
Love Requires Trust,
Performance Implies Distrust

———————————————————

"Here's an uncomfortable truth for women, especially those of us auditioning for a man's love: If you can't be yourself with him, then deep down, either you don't trust him, or you don't trust yourself. Sometimes both."
—from the journal of Umm Zakiyyah

"True intimacy comes from vulnerability, and vulnerability comes from authenticity."
—Vanessa Ooms, *Do It For You: How to Stop People-Pleasing and Find Peace*

53

True Love Requires Trust and Emotional Safety

"I feel safe with my partner because:
1. He would never ever ever be the source of harm that I'm trying
to avoid. This is by far the most important thing.
2. I'm able to emotionally open up without fear of being
misunderstood or too quickly judged. He'll always hear out my
side of things, and if he disagrees, then we can have a respectful
debate about the topic.
3. There's a stability to our relationship. He's not going to
suddenly stop loving me or stop being kind to me...
Essentially, feeling safe with your partner just means that you trust
them."
—commenter on Reddit thread, "What does feeling 'safe' with
your partner mean to you?"

A woman who has embodied true femininity feels emotionally safe enough to show up as she truly is. This is the case whether she is an extrovert or an introvert, an adventurer or a recluse, a homemaker or businesswoman, or some composite of them all.

Furthermore, a woman who has embodied true femininity is not held back by external pressures or even by her own external appearance, nor is she propelled forward by it. This is because she lives in a space of inner trust wherein her beauty radiates from her inside out, not outside in.

When it comes to seeking love and the soul companionship of marriage, a woman who has embodied femininity trusts that she will connect with a man who appreciates all the unique traits and experiences that make up who she is as a person (as she will do for him). This is in sharp contrast to the woman living in the wounded feminine and thus anxiously seeks the approval and praise of a man who values only women who show up as a cookie-cutter prototype of a "high value woman."

Additionally, a woman who has embodied femininity might have reached a stage in her personal life and emotional development where, at least at this juncture in her journey, she is not seeking marriage at all.

This woman will likely be prioritizing healing her childhood wounds (especially an underlying father wound) before seeking a relationship with a man. This is because she knows that without this inner healing, nearly all men will feel unsafe to her nervous system. (And when I say she is prioritizing "healing," I mean she is seeking to become healed *enough*, as being completely and flawlessly healed isn't possible in the human experience).

For this reason, she delays seeking marriage because she knows that if she does seek love and companionship in her unhealed state—and while feeling unsafe and unloved within herself—this lack of safety and self-love will likely inspire her to anxiously perform for love, instead of trusting herself and her intuition to both recognize healthy love when it arrives and to calmly receive it and fully let it in.

54

Performing Femininity Is About Distrusting Yourself and Men

Women who perform femininity tend to think of men as a monolith who value all the same things in women and who dislike all the same things in women. Therefore, these women tend to interact with men from a space of anxiousness, insecurity, and fear—which really amounts to deep distrust of men, especially regarding a man's ability (or willingness) to appreciate the various complexities of each woman as a unique soul and personality.

Unfortunately, once these women have deeply internalized their distrust of men and themselves, they perceive their conclusions about life and love as some sort of esoteric "inner wisdom" that other women need to understand in order to "become more feminine." If these unhealed women have been married for years in emotionally unsafe relationships—and have thus become experts in staying stuck in "survival mode" (as so many of us have at some point in our lives)—they'll count the fact that they never chose divorce as proof that they understand "what it takes to make a marriage work."

So, they eagerly offer advice to other women, especially those whom they perceive as unable to keep a relationship together. Meanwhile, the very woman they deem as unsuccessful in marriage is likely on a divinely blessed journey of healing and self-honesty. Thus, this self-honest woman recognizes that for the sake of her wellbeing and safety, it is exponentially wiser and more beneficial to her soul to remain single for the rest of her life than to agree to the type of toxic relationship that the "wise married woman" who is stuck in performing femininity is inviting (or shaming) her into.

Healed Women Admire Wellness, Not Toxic Stability

A woman who is emotionally healed and has embodied true femininity—like a man who has emotionally healed and encapsulates taqwaa-centered manhood—doesn't look solely at people's external relationship status or the numerical number assigned to the time they've been together to determine whether or not their lifestyle choices are worthy of emulating.

Rather, these emotionally healed, spiritually mature women and men look at a man and woman's alignment with foundational and spiritual principles of a healthy marriage. They also look at how that couple actually experiences their relationship individually and as a unit, both externally and internally—emotionally, mentally, and spiritually—in the presence of themselves and each other.

In other words, when we have a healthy sense of self, we begin to intuitively understand what a healthy relationship looks like. In this space, we begin to understand what it means to nurture a marriage that *truly* works, which includes (amongst other things) each person prioritizing their and their companion's wellness—emotionally, mentally, physically, and spiritually.

Therefore, how long a particular couple was able to, for example, avoid serving divorce papers to the other person is less important than how deeply each person feels safe, loved, and joyful in the relationship and in the other person's presence. Furthermore, how inspired both people— husband *and* wife—genuinely feel to grow into the best version of themselves is of crucial importance in assessing the health and vitality of a relationship.

Toxic Stability

"This is what so many of us are rejoicing in and seeking contentment in—a life of ease and relative calm because we are unwilling to take a single risk that could disrupt the comfortable toxicity of our life.

So, we stay in unhealthy relationships and religious groups, and then count it as a favor from Allah that we are not suffering the trials that befall those who fight daily for the health of their hearts and souls.

So, we watch them go through test after test in the path of self-betterment and emotional healing, and we think, 'Had they remained with us (i.e., doing what we do), they wouldn't be going through all that.'

If only they stayed married
If only they followed our sheikh
If only they remained silent on such and such issue
If only they kept better ties with their family...

Thereby imagining we are being granted some immense divine favor for the quiet contentment we enjoy, due to never braving our own internal battles of life and soul."

—from the journal of Umm Zakiyyah

55

Trust Men's Inner Experience, But Not Women's?

When we perform femininity and thus distrust a man's ability or willingness to care about *our* inner experiences and unique needs, then we begin to rely heavily on trusting what a man *says* about men's inner experiences and needs in reaction to how women show up.

As a result, we carefully (and sometimes obsessively) study what a random man says about women (negatively or positively), then we consistently show up in the "positive way" that he alluded to. Then if we begin to genuinely feel that any of this is negatively impacting us (or our current relationship), we dismiss our own thoughts and feelings, choosing to instead focus all our energy in following a random man's script of what he *says* a good relationship must be.

Performing Femininity Makes Us Distrust Women

Women who consistently abandon themselves do so because they genuinely feel the *need* to perform femininity in order to win (or secure) a man's love. Whenever we engage in this type of self-betrayal, there is a deep knowing inside of us that says: *This man does not care about me, and he will not prioritize what I need from him. So, it's best to focus on caretaking him and prioritizing what he needs (or desires) from me.*

225

Because of this internalized "wounded feminine" mindset, it is commonplace for women (especially those deeply invested in performing femininity) to accept as truth what men say women are doing wrong in relationships. However, they consistently reject and find fault in what women say *men* are doing wrong in relationships.

For example, if a man says that a woman should always dress in sexy (or at least attractive) clothing for her husband and stop wearing raggedy sweatpants and food-stained shirts at home, women who perform femininity will eagerly agree with him and rush to share this "sage wisdom" with women they think need to hear it. And while the advice itself isn't technically wrong or problematic—and is actually quite beneficial—here is where the fault lines begin to show:

On the other hand, if a woman says men should always prioritize a woman's financial security and her ability to maximize rest and self-care at home (e.g., through her husband paying for in-house help, even if a maid comes only once a month), women who perform femininity will rush to remind women of this "sage wisdom" for "good wives," especially the modern-day Western "good girl" culture's version of it:

If you're truly a feminine woman, you'll take care of *all* of the cooking, cleaning, and childcare all by yourself. (Interestingly, Muslims uphold this mentality even though in prophetic history, it was standard for women to have help in the home). Then after a long day of cooking cleaning, and childcare, you'll also rush to serve and please your husband when he comes home, and you'll have absolutely no needs or desires that require *him* to level up in how he shows up for you.

Here, it is relevant to note that we as women (and men) can (and should) strive our level best to get the support we ourselves need—whether through therapy for our emotional challenges or through help from family and friends for daily household tasks and childcare—so that we can show up as the best wives (and husbands) while utilizing the resources that are reasonably available and affordable to us.

Good Advice Is Good Advice, But It Goes Both Ways

The point here isn't that the perspective that men share about their relationship needs is invalid. In fact, much of it is most certainly valid, especially regarding how women present themselves physically at home. Rather the point here is that when women share *equally* valid perspectives about *their* needs, the female point of view is routinely dismissed, denied, or trivialized—unless it happens to align with what these same men are already saying about women.

56

Prioritizing a Woman's Joy, Comfort, and Wellness Can Save a Relationship

If we go back to the aforementioned example about the importance of men investing in a woman's financial security while maximizing her opportunity for rest and self-care in the home, the truth is that, *every* woman—even those performing femininity instead of embodying it—is *more* able to serve and please her husband when she isn't physically and emotionally depleted at the end of the day. Yet this is what happens when women are taking care of children from sunrise to bedtime and completing endless chores with minimal rest and no help.

The truth is, every woman is better able to focus on, and thus prioritize, what her husband needs from her if she herself isn't stressed about a long to-do list or endless financial problems every day. Moreover, if this lack of stress includes investment in things that bring her joy, she is all the more able to fulfill her duties at home and in her relationship with her husband.

In an article entitled "Speaking of Health: Tips for embracing joy in daily life," Mayo Clinic Health System states:

> "Joy is a powerful emotion and harnessing it can be a remedy for stress-related burnout. Contentment and joy can positively improve physical and mental health and

overall well-being" (mayoclinichealthsystem.org; March 23, 2023).

Yet still, in the vast majority of discussions surrounding what it means to be a "feminine woman," it is the man's joy, needs, and standards about how a woman should show up that are amplified and thus prioritized. In this space, it is rare (or non-existent) that a woman's internal world of joy, needs, and standards regarding a man's masculinity is amplified or prioritized.

This is the case even when a woman is speaking *only* about masculinity from the perspective of a man investing in what would increase the likelihood of him getting *his* needs met.

Hard-Learned Lessons in Performative Womanhood

So, we learn that in the world of performing for love, the only inner experience worth focusing on in hopes of building a lasting relationship is that of the man. In contrast, in the world of embodying our authenticity in femininity (and masculinity), there is a mutual desire and motivation to prioritize not only what we ourselves need from ourselves, but also what our soul companion needs or desires from us.

57

Performing Femininity Fuels Hypervigilance and Centers Unrighteous Men

When performing femininity is prioritized over embodying femininity, women are constantly on the lookout for what they are "doing wrong" in a relationship (and what they could be doing better), instead of on how they can show up more authentically for themselves and in the relationship. This is because performing femininity is based on an external system of measurement that has nothing at all to do with a woman's own needs, desires, and life circumstance—or even with the unique needs, desires, and circumstances of her relationship itself.

While nearly all women can certainly benefit from advice and resources that highlight general baselines that tend to apply to *most* men, performing femininity isn't about general baselines. It is about adhering to very specific behavior—or to very specific ideas—about your inherently high or low "value" to a man. This heavily scripted behavior is designed to win the love, commitment, or approval of a specific type of man (or a very specific group of men)—often without having had a single honest conversation with these men themselves.

However, even in cases where certain advice tends to accurately highlight what most men value in women, this accuracy alone doesn't mean that this general truth is one that women should lean toward or focus on. This is because of the simple fact that what is true for *most* people (male or female) is not necessarily true for most *sincere*, God-fearing men and women, especially those who prioritize taqwaa as a lifestyle.

Thus, when it comes to men who are emotionally healed and whose character and deen encapsulate taqwaa-centered manhood, what *they* like or desire in a woman is likely going to differ greatly from the "majority of men." This is because any tool of measurement that centers a surface level "performance review" from a general majority will rarely if ever include the mindset of genuinely good men, who tend to live outside the majority mentality of the collective wounded masculine.

RE-CAP

Review of Essentials

Compassionate Accountability Prompts
for Embodying Femininity

1. Look deep within and be honest with yourself:
   Do you trust yourself—emotionally, intimately, and/or spiritually? Why or why not? If not, what is one small step you can take to begin building that self-trust? (For example, if you distrust yourself spiritually because you struggle to pray on time or because you sometimes miss prayers, one small step you can take is this: Plan your daily schedule around your Salaah instead of trying to fit in your Salaah around your daily schedule.)

2. If you are married, answer this question as honestly as you feel emotionally safe and mentally ready to now: **Do you trust your husband—emotionally, intimately, and/or spiritually?** Why or why not? If

not, what is one small step you can take to begin building that trust between you? (For example, in a space of love and compassion and when the moment is right, share with your husband one good thing that you normally would keep to yourself, even if it seems small, like something that made you smile today; and/or share with him one thing you love about him or one thing that you're extremely grateful to him for. These tiny moments of "daring to trust" can begin to shift your own inner world, to expand the compassion between you and your husband, and to soften the emotional energy in your relationship.)

3. Take in a deep breath and exhale slowly, then in a space of mental calm, ask yourself these questions: **What brings me the most joy or comfort in life? When do I feel most "alive" and most like myself? When do I feel the most grateful and excited about life or love?**

REASON TEN
Love and Unsafety Cannot Coexist

―――――――――――――――

"By the time you're consciously considering whether something [or someone] is safe, dangerous, or threatening, your body has already made a decision."
―Aurianna Joy and Will Rezin, Trauma and Somatics Course

"While there are definitely things a person can do to help their partner feel safe, feeling safe consists of two parts: having a healthy external environment and having a healthy internal environment...
It isn't solely on the other person to 'make you feel safe'; it's also an inside job."
―Sheleana Aiyana, *Becoming the One: Heal Your Past, Transform Your Relationship Patterns, and Come Home to Yourself*

58

They Need to Constantly Feel Superior, Not Safe to You

When I was a young girl, I learned that during any unexpected (and often unintentional) disagreement with a man or older boy (or sometimes even a younger boy), it was always safer to at least pretend to agree with him. So, I learned to stuff down my feelings and to almost always center a male's emotional "needs"—which often just meant restlessly ensuring that no male soul ever experienced the inner discomfort of being "wrong," especially in front of an insignificant "little girl" like myself.

Over time, I learned to almost instinctively acquiesce to a male's needs, demands, or expectations, even before he verbalized them or made them known—and even when it was unclear whether or not he himself was consciously aware of these.

Before I had the words to convey what I was sensing, I learned early on that boys and men need to constantly feel "superior" to girls and women. I also learned that it was my job as a female soul in this world to constantly shrink myself on their behalf so as to ensure that they maintained a constant feeling of superiority. Moreover, I learned that it was essentially a woman's God-given role in life to make men feel strong, smart, and powerful at all times, even when the opposite was painfully obvious—or *especially* when the opposite was painfully obvious.

Protecting Myself from Harm

From repeated hurtful experiences during my youth, I learned that trying to be a voice of reason during these moments could lead to suffering verbal attacks, withstanding vicious insults, or even sustaining physical harm.

As a result, I became hypervigilant to any signs that I had inadvertently hurt a man's feelings, that I'd unintentionally made him feel "small" in any way, or that I'd made him think I had more knowledge or experience than he did (even if I actually did).

These repeated experiences were my first lessons in what would remain a lifelong rule-of-thumb for interacting with men: *Men need to feel constantly superior to women, not genuinely safe for women.*

59

We Need to Stay Small and Unthreatening, Not Safe or Protected

It wasn't until I embarked on my own journey of healing and self-accountability that I realized that by anxiously adhering to the aforementioned rule of thumb in my interactions with men, I was living in my own wounded feminine. This wounding made me see the needs and desires of men as defined primarily by the collective wounded masculine instead of by Allah's divinely assigned *qawwaamah*. Yet this divine assignment of safe, compassionate leadership and protection of women's safety and holistic wellness is taqwaa-centered manhood itself. Thus, it is the only authentic masculinity that exists.

When we are living in our wounded feminine as women, we might *think* we understand *qawwaamah* and spiritual femininity, but our addiction to obsessive people-pleasing and emotional self-abandonment betrays the truth of what is really going on with us. Our disconnect from our own unique needs, desires, and holistic wellness in this world incites us to listen anxiously and attentively to the loudest and most unhealed of men in this world. It is as students of the collective wounded masculine that we learn the meaning and proofs of our own femininity.

From these men who take pride in their unwellness and unhealed states, we learn that we must stay small and unthreatening to their fragile egos, which are prone to collapse at the slightest reminder that they aren't showing up as they should. At the same time, in our own unwellness and unhealed states, we claim that these same (allegedly) strong "real men" are keeping us safe and protected in this world.

In other words, we intuitively know that these unhealed men do not have the capacity to show up for us in any meaningful way (other than, for example, providing us with financial provision). So, instead, we show up for *them* in a way that makes these men *feel* they are doing a great job at performing manhood.

Power Plays, Victimhood, and Entitlement

"By default, performative womanhood and performative manhood are about each person's commitment to disconnecting from their own inner world and their own self-accountability. So, at its core, performing femininity is about consistently showing up in victimhood and helplessness, and performing masculinity is about consistently showing up in power-play and entitlement. Yet beneath each show of victimhood is a power-play, and beneath each show of helplessness is entitlement. Similarly, beneath each power-play is victimhood, and beneath each show of entitlement is helplessness. This is because both the man and the woman are using their performative roles to control the other person and the outcome of a situation while simultaneously pretending it's solely the other person's responsibility to make any necessary changes."
—from the journal of Umm Zakiyyah

60

We Become Experts at Self-Protection Because Our Men Don't See Us

By the time I was a teenager, I was effectively an expert at preemptively protecting myself from male harm—even if it resulted in my own harm. This included being overly nice, even to strangers who made me feel unsafe, and pretending to enjoy unwanted attention, even when I was terrified for my life or safety. This latter tendency was one that, unfortunately, carried over into seriously entertaining marrying men who obviously couldn't offer me healthy love, as is the case for so many women.

In my own life, I've come to describe the inner experience of my nervous system in these cases as being constantly "in search of no." When it afflicts women, this "in search of no" phenomenon translates into a woman saying yes to a relationship or circumstance with a man even though deep down she has no desire to be in that relationship or circumstance with him.

For example, in this state you might say yes to a romantic relationship (including marriage itself), to giving a man your phone number, or to being in a compromising situation even when deep down you desperately desire a way out of this situation. However, because we see no way out, we say yes because we genuinely don't know *how* to say no—or because we don't know how to say no safely. This lack of safety is exponentially increased when there is additional pressure from your family, your culture, your faith community, or society at large to be in a relationship with a man or to perpetually acquiesce to the desires of men as proof of your femininity.

What makes this phenomenon all the more destructive and pervasive is that this added external pressure in an already uncomfortable or dangerous situation doesn't have to be intentional or even actively present at the time. In other words, the "good girl" programming that is at the root of performing femininity ultimately becomes a psychological constant for girls and women.

This is because since childhood year after year (and generation after generation) we have heard that good girls do what they are told and that *smart* good girls don't make boys (or men) angry. We also learn that good girls who refuse to obey without question or who avoid humbly submitting to powerful men in authority (even those who terrify them or harm them) will earn the curse of God in this world and His painful punishment in the Hereafter.

Ultimately, we internalize these terrifying messages until they live in us every second of the day. And you can't just turn off your inner "knowing" at will, even if it's in your best interest to do so.

Unfortunately, the most heartbreaking part of all of this is that on an unconscious level, we are operating with this belief: *We say yes to male harm because we've learned that pleasing a man who is more powerful (and more important) than we are is our greatest chance at self-protection and survival.*

241

61

We Learn to Smile When We Want to Cry and Agree When We Want to Say No

By the time I was a young adult, I avoided displaying even the slightest signs of open disagreement or anger in reaction to men, even when they were openly disagreeing with me and even when they were relentlessly unleashing *their* anger onto me.

As a young woman, it was profoundly confusing navigating this existence, especially since my religion and Holy Book told me that these men had been divinely assigned as my protectors in this world. Meanwhile I found myself constantly feeling like it was my divine assignment to protect *them*, most especially from ever seeing themselves, from ever taking accountability for themselves or their behavior, and from genuinely understanding how much I needed them to protect *me*.

Over time, I figured I'd misunderstood my religion and Holy Book all along. Maybe God only wanted women to make men *feel* like they were sources of safety and protection for women, yet it was women's job to be sources of safety and protection for themselves (and each other). And after we got married, if we did such a good job of pulling this off that our husbands were deeply pleased with how manly we made them feel (even if they failed terribly in how they made *us* feel as women), then God's eternal pleasure and Paradise was ours.

Consequently, I began to embrace my role in performative womanhood as if it was God's work itself. Meanwhile, I had no idea I was living in wounded femininity seeking to please and appease men living in wounded masculinity.

So, in my efforts to make men feel manly, I learned that certain topics were completely off limits in male company, and I learned that the most dangerous of these topics was anything related to their manhood.

I also learned this unspoken rule: Men could talk endlessly about what women should or shouldn't be doing, and it was our obligation to humbly listen and show up in the ways they said they wanted or needed us to. But women couldn't talk about what men should or shouldn't be doing (at least not without the risk of being called out of our names). And a woman most certainly couldn't (and shouldn't) expect a man with an ounce of "manhood" to actually listen to her or take her seriously. Why? Because "real men" don't listen to women. Instead, they command so much power and authority over their wives and children that they inspire every single one of them to humbly obey and listen to them.

All of these lessons from childhood and young adulthood taught me this additional lesson: *More than anything, men need to feel superior to women; however, men actually keeping women safe from harm is not necessarily included in this superiority or divine assignment.*

Or so I thought.

62

He Only Wants Good Food, Good Sex, and Quiet Submission

In this path of performative womanhood, we learn that other than paying for our food, clothing, and shelter; our men can't (or won't) show up for us in this world—that is, if they are *truly* strong and manly, as defined by the performative existences we prefer most in our unhealed states. This is because to the unhealed nafs, men's weighty responsibility to the world is too grand and far too important to waste time on "women's issues" or even on women themselves.

So, as women we learn that our desires and needs are at best frivolous to men and at worst harmful hindrances to them. This is because we (and they) imagine that tending to women's needs prevents them from fulfilling their most imperative duty of saving and running the world.

Once we internalize these messages, we begin to believe that men won't ever genuinely *see* us as women, whether we are their wives and daughters or we are their sisters in faith and humanity. Consequently, we tell ourselves that we can't (or at least shouldn't) expect them to genuinely care about us or our needs, or to even protect us from harm—not even from their own harm. In fact, we tell ourselves that if we are *really* good wives and daughters, then we quietly and humbly accept whatever harm our husbands or fathers unleash on us in the home.

In the world of performing femininity, this is how wise, good women (and daughters) learn to protect themselves from harm while also making their husbands and fathers feel like the strongest, most powerful men in the world. Meanwhile, many of these women and girls are the *most* terrified of the harm they suffer at the hands of the men who were divinely assigned as their protectors and guardians in this world.

By the time many of us get married, we have already internalized the following belief, even if only unconsciously: The *less* a woman seeks emotional connection with her man and the *less* she seeks genuine safety and protection from him, the *more* pious and righteous she is in his eyes and the *more* cherished she is to him. This is because in the world of performing femininity, sincere God-fearing women ask nothing from their men and expect even *less* than that from them. Therefore, these "good women" leave their men alone and focus on giving their husbands the only three things that "real men" care about: good food, good sex, and a woman who quietly does what she's told.

But Do You Feel Emotionally Safe with Him?

"The deepest need of the female soul is to feel safe and protected in a space of compassion and empathy. This allows her to relax into her spiritual feminine and pour life and love into the world around her."
—from the journal of Umm Zakiyyah

"…when our anxiety is high and our confidence is low, we may become externally focused and fixate on being wanted rather than paying attention to what is going on inside of us…[Then] when our wounds are triggered, we naturally believe the person we're fixated on is the solution to our pain."
—Sheleana Aiyana, *Becoming the One: Heal Your Past, Transform Your Relationship Patterns, and Come Home to Yourself*

63

The Dangers of Submission Before Safety

Performing femininity requires a woman to submit fully to a man before she feels emotionally safe in his presence. Whenever a feminine soul forces herself to continuously relax, trust, and surrender to masculine energy despite feeling unsafe in a man's presence, she trains herself to override her intuition in exchange for male approval. She also teaches herself that her needs and desires don't matter, only a man's do.

A female soul doesn't feel unsafe due to only obvious danger or intentional harm. If a female soul consistently feels unheard and unseen, especially in the "safe container" of marriage, or if she knows deep down that her needs and desires are not a priority to the one who was divinely assigned to protect her and keep her safe from harm (starting with her own father and mother), then deep inside, she will *feel* unsafe—even if there is no obvious threat to her safety in real-time.

In fact, a man's (or parent's) mere indifference to a woman's emotional needs—especially if this indifference is generally more consistent than his sincere and compassionate attentiveness—is enough to incite feelings of unsafety in the female nervous system.

While a sincere, righteous woman will likely push herself to submit—even when she feels unsafe—it comes at a hefty cost to her overall wellbeing. The feeling of unsafety in the female nafs is not a conscious decision on the woman's part; it is merely how the Creator designed her inner world in response to feeling unseen, unprotected, or threatened. So, if a woman continues to force herself to submit even in the face of what feels like danger to her nafs, her nervous system will work overtime just to allow her to function in this environment of unsafety each day.

Eventually, the woman's overworked nervous system will cause her body and soul to become exhausted and her mind to become fogged with confusion and disarray. This inner experience will then likely incite both emotional and spiritual wounding to the deepest part of her existence—her nafs.

If even still, she continues to push herself to "perform femininity" in these circumstances, especially if she is motivated mostly by a fear of displeasing her husband or of sinfulness in front of God, then over time, she will likely become afflicted with pervasive unwellness that negatively affects her mental and spiritual health, as well as her physical wellness.

Prophet Muhammad (peace and blessings be upon him) himself cautioned both men and women against placing undue stress on the body while also highlighting the fact that women have rights over their husbands in marriage: "Your body has a right over you, your eyes have a right over you and your wife has a right over you" (Sahih al-Bukhari, 5199). So, it is upon each and every son and daughter of Adam to take care of their bodies as well as their souls, and it is upon every husband to tend to the emotional and intimate needs of his wife.

64

Being a "Good Woman" Almost Killed Her

When our definitions of being a "good woman" go to the extreme, we are not only risking our physical health, but we are also placing our very lives in danger.

In emphasizing the dangers of this sort of self-sacrificial lifestyle in women, Dr. Gabor Maté in a video entitled "How Being Too Nice Can Destroy You" tells the story of a woman whose stress levels elevated so much that she was diagnosed with stage four breast cancer at only 37 years old. He said that by the time she was diagnosed, the cancer was already in her bones, and she was given only one year to live.

What made her case so shocking to those around her was that she was physically fit, had a cheerful disposition and was known as a devoted mother and wife. She was married to a wealthy businessman and also enjoyed her own financial success. To nearly everyone around, "she had it all."

However, the problem was, she was striving so hard to show up for others that she ended up sacrificing who she really was to be who others needed her to be. Her life turned around only after she began to healthily center her own needs, which included walking away from commitments she'd made to others and also talking to her husband about things she had suppressed for years. This saved her life.

Dr. Gabor Maté said, "She knows that if she wants to stay alive, she needs to stay authentic" (Your Inner Child Matters; September 10, 2023).

Additionally, the "sensitive" nature of women makes them more prone to autoimmune diseases in comparison to men. This risk significantly increases when cortisol, the body's stress hormone, is in excessive amounts in the body, which is what happens when a person's nervous system feels unsafe.

Practically speaking, what this means is that women's biology requires gentleness in that their most intimate relationships should be a source of emotional safety for them. If they do not receive this emotional safety, their very physical health and, ultimately, their life is compromised. This is how Allah created women on a chromosomal level:

> "The larger number of genes originating from the X chromosome creates a far greater possibility of a larger number of mutations occurring. This puts women at a greater risk for the development of autoimmune diseases solely due to women having two X chromosomes, whereas men possess only one. The presence of two X chromosomes essentially creates a 'double dose' of genes present on the X chromosome and because of this, predisposes the female to autoimmunity" (Angum F. et al, 2020).

One article summarized this phenomenon in its title: "'Nice people' more likely to get autoimmune diseases; women even more." It says:

> "When raising kids, especially girls, our value system teaches us to always be 'nice' or 'good' to others. However, always being nice and kind to other people may do you more harm than good...The doctor explained that going along with a 'socially determined role' of putting others before themselves and repressing anger leads to

generating stress unconsciously. This buildup of stress 'invites' such illnesses" (Aug 26, 2023).

65

Men Set the Temperature of a Relationship, Women Nurture It

So much of what we are witnessing today in our unhealthy relationships and "failing marriages" is the result of unhealed men (some who are sincere and well-intentioned) trying to "straighten women out" instead of being her safe space, especially when she is hurting. Yet in a famous hadith Prophet Muhammad (peace be upon him), said:

> **"I enjoin you to treat women well, for the woman was created from a rib and the most curved part of the rib is its highest point. If you try to straighten it, you will break it. If you leave it as it is, it will remain bent. Thus, I enjoin you to be good to women"** (Sahih Bukhari 2153 and Sahih Muslim 1468).

Here it is relevant to mention something that even many non-Muslim relationship advisors routinely point out: So long as a woman is venting to *you*, she still has in her heart some level of trust for you (or at least hope for trust) that you can be a safe space for her. So, when she is in front of you opening her heart to you, please try to hear her hurting heart more than you hear her hurtful words. And when you listen, listen with your own heart in a place of gentleness instead of harshness.

Dealing gently with people, especially women, opens the door to meaningful connection and healing while dealing with them harshly causes them to break away from you and find safety and compassion elsewhere.

In the Qur'an, Allah says,

فَبِمَا رَحْمَةٍ مِّنَ ٱللَّهِ لِنتَ لَهُمْ وَلَوْ كُنتَ فَظًّا غَلِيظَ ٱلْقَلْبِ لَٱنفَضُّواْ مِنْ حَوْلِكَ فَٱعْفُ عَنْهُمْ وَٱسْتَغْفِرْ لَهُمْ وَشَاوِرْهُمْ فِي ٱلْأَمْرِ فَإِذَا عَزَمْتَ فَتَوَكَّلْ عَلَى ٱللَّهِ إِنَّ ٱللَّهَ يُحِبُّ ٱلْمُتَوَكِّلِينَ ﴿١٥٩﴾

"And by the Mercy of Allah, you dealt with them gently. And had you been rude [in speech] and harsh-hearted, they would have broken away from about you.
So, pass over (their faults), and ask (Allah's) Forgiveness for them; and consult them in the affairs. Then when you have taken a decision, put your trust in Allah. Certainly, Allah loves those who put their trust (in Him)."
—*Ali 'Imraan* (3:159)

To understand how serious this all is on a biological level in the human being—most especially in the woman given the aforementioned chromosomal and autoimmune research findings—Daniel Goleman, in his book *Social Intelligence*, explains how even the most ostensibly trivial interactions with each other can affect a person's brain, emotions, and physical health:

"Even our most routine encounters act as regulators in the brain, priming our emotions, some desirable, others not… These [social interactions, even if brief] take on a deep consequence as we realize how, through their sum total, we create one another" (2006.)

What we can understand from this is that widely circulated sayings like the one by Tony Evans— *"Men, you are a thermostat…Your job is to set the temperature"*— are not just witty quotes. They are biological and emotional facts, facts that directly impact a woman's overall wellbeing and feelings of emotional safety in a relationship.

In the book *The Man's Guide to Women: Scientifically Proven Secrets from the Love Lab*, author John Gottman, PhD (founder of the famous Gottman Institute) and his coauthors say:

> "Research shows that what men do in a relationship is, by a large margin, the crucial factor that separates a great relationship from a failed one. This does not mean that a woman doesn't need to do her part, but the data proves that a man's actions are the key variable that determines whether a relationship succeeds or fails" (2016).

While it most certainly is the responsibility of both the man and the woman to ensure an emotionally healthy "temperature" in a marriage, a woman can only *maintain* or *build upon* (i.e., nurture and nourish) the emotional foundation that her leader and protector has already set. So, if her *qawwaam* never established emotional safety in the home to begin with, the woman has absolutely nothing to healthily build upon, let alone nurture.

Of course, how a woman shows up can also potentially disrupt the compassionate foundation that her husband has laid, but he first has to lay this safe foundation in the first place. Then it is only in an environment of emotional safety that a woman's inner world allows her to surrender and submit.

It Feels Good to Let Him Lead

"If you have someone in your life where you don't feel safe or you don't feel protected, you're not going to open. In a relationship that has masculine and feminine polarity, a woman needs to feel safe. She needs to trust in herself and her choices and honor that and honor her boundaries. She can be open and express to be wild and carefree. We want a man to hold our energy, so we feel safe and express ourself. That's where our feminine…power comes from — within. We need to be careful in choosing someone that we really, really trust and that we can lean into their arms and know we are safe.
When we lean back and let him lead, we in turn get to get our power back. *This is because we're not mothering him. We're not telling him what to do. We're not in the control.* ***We can let go because we know he's got our back*** *and that's the most powerful feeling for a woman — to feel loved, adored, cherished, protected, seen, and heard."*
—Angela Rose, "What Women Need to Feel Safe in a Relationship"

66

Feelings of Safety Inspire Surrender and Submission

When a woman feels safe, she relaxes, she trusts, and she surrenders. It really is that simple. This process of relaxing, trusting, and surrendering is often called leaning into our feminine energy. But it is even more so a manifestation of the deepest fitrah (inherent nature) of the female soul.

Our Merciful, All-Wise Rabb created the female nafs (her deep, inner self) such that a strong, compassionate masculine presence naturally makes a woman feel safe from the depths of her heart and soul. So, if a woman struggles to relax, trust, and surrender, this isn't in itself a sign that she isn't pious or "feminine." It also isn't a sign that she needs to work harder at being "submissive." It is merely a sign that her nafs doesn't yet feel safe enough to "let go" such that her inner protective walls are no longer needed.

A Woman's Unsafety Isn't Always a Man's Fault

While a female soul's lack of safety isn't always a man's fault, providing an environment that is safe enough for a woman to relax, trust, and surrender is *always* a man's responsibility. This divinely assigned role—often referred to as *qawwaamah* in Arabic—is most evident in the privacy of the marital home, but it also extends to the community space of a woman's spiritual home.

So, when we find more and more women displaying traits that so many call "un-feminine," the root cause is generally not in the woman herself but in the unsafe environment(s) that she has been forced to live and survive.

Therefore, the solution is for our leaders and protectors—our *qawwaamoon*—to work harder at creating safe spaces for female souls, both privately and publicly.

However, when our leaders and protectors continuously demand women's trust and submission before they offer any meaningful safety to female souls, then it is in a woman's nature to increasingly feel more and more unsafe in male company—even if that male company is primarily her husband.

Yes, as aforementioned, a sincere, "righteous wife" will certainly work hard at relaxing, trusting, and surrendering to her husband regardless of how she feels internally. However, if day after day, she continuously forces herself to submit to "male authority" before she feels genuinely safe to, it is only a matter of time before her nafs—her inner world of body, mind, and soul—collapses in on itself.

This collapse isn't due to impiety or even conscious choice on a woman's part. Rather it is due to the inherent nature of a female soul constantly living in survival mode.

67

Performing Femininity Disconnects You from Female Pleasure

Have you ever heard of **sensual femininity**? This is when a woman feels so deeply connected to her soul companion that she begins to look forward to intimate "sexploration" with her husband. But you can't enjoy true, deep pleasurable intimacy if you don't feel emotionally safe in your marriage. However, sensual femininity is so much more than sex.

Healthy intimacy is rooted in a level of intimacy that begins first with a deep emotional connection rooted in emotional safety. A woman embodies healthy sensual femininity only in the presence of consistent safe masculine energy that is:

✓ strong and protective
✓ gentle and compassionate
✓ validating and nourishing

A woman who is blessed with safe masculine energy feels seen, heard, and cherished. In safe masculine energy, the female soul feels more and more inspired to grow and become the best version of herself—personally, emotionally, and spiritually.

Whenever you perform femininity instead of embody femininity, it is most likely due to feeling unsafe in the masculine energy around you. So, you never feel truly safe enough to embrace true, healthy sensuality.

Here's the bottom line: As long as you are performing femininity instead of embodying it, you will <u>never</u> experience true female pleasure, at least not with any meaningful consistency. In your "performance role" your pleasurable sexual experiences will be primarily biological (enjoyed mainly because your body craved sex), sporadic (because you can't predict when your body will feel safe enough to relax and enjoy itself), or pleasurable on only a surface level (because you're unable to fully "let go" enough to enjoy all the levels of intimate pleasure that your female body has been created to experience).

RE-CAP

Reason 10
Why Performing Femininity Never Works in Love

●━━━━━━━━━━━━━━━━━━━━●

Love and unsafety cannot coexist in a healthy, loving relationship. Yet performing femininity often happens precisely because we don't feel emotionally safe to show up as ourselves.

Compassionate Accountability Prompts
for Embodying Femininity

1. **Do you feel safe with yourself—emotionally, physically, and spiritually?** In other words, do you feel loved, validated, and honored in your relationship with yourself? Are your mind, body, and soul safe spaces for you? Are they sources of self-compassion? Are they sources of soul-nourishing gratitude? And are they sources of loving accountability? If so, how so? If not, why not?

2. If you don't feel safe and loved within your own mind, body, or soul (as mentioned in number 1), what are some of your earliest memories of feeling this mental, physical, or spiritual unsafety? **In what ways have traces of these unsafe feelings spilled into your relationships today?** In what ways have they shaped your personal understanding of being a "good

woman," having a successful marriage, or being a "good Muslim" and having strong faith?

3. **If you are married, do you feel a deep sense of safety with your husband**—emotionally, physically, sexually, and spiritually? Do you feel completely free to be yourself in his presence? Do you feel the most loved, appreciated, and cherished the more joyful, honest, and authentic you are? If so, how so? If not, why not?

4. In a space of mental and emotional calm, write or speak this affirmation of emotional safety three times: *I am safe. I am loved. Allah is with me.*

5. For this last question, respond <u>only if</u> you sense that, deep down, it is relevant to your own life and choices *and* if you feel emotionally safe to answer right now:

    Why do I keep *choosing* unsafety?

    Remember, this isn't about self-blame, it's about self-awareness. **It is <u>not</u> your fault what happened to you, so you shouldn't blame yourself for it,** especially if it happened in childhood. Instead, get curious about the reasons behind your poor choices as an adult (e.g., emotional wounding, nervous system dysregulation, unresolved childhood trauma, spiritual crisis, etc.), especially if you are making these poor choices unintentionally. And keep in mind that **choosing something is not the same as consciously *wanting* it or purposely *seeking* it.**

    NOTE: If you feel deeply triggered, angered, or victimized by the question, do <u>not</u> respond to it, at least not right now. **Angry feelings are a natural, necessary, and healthy reaction to having been continuously harmed, wronged, or traumatized,** especially if the people around you trivialized or denied any of your painful experiences. **It is how you**

handle these angry feelings that reflects the dividing line between emotional wellness and emotional harm. Additionally, feeling emotionally triggered, angered, or victimized is often a sign that your very real hurtful experiences have not yet been validated, or have not yet been validated *enough*.

In that case, your priority should be to find a safe compassionate witness who will listen without judgment to what happened to you and then empathetically validate what you experienced. If possible, this can be a mental health professional or a support group. However, a deeply empathetic, trustworthy friend can suffice. (Just be sure to first ask their permission before sharing, as your story could be too emotionally overwhelming or triggering for them. Then if they agree to listen, let them know that you need a compassionate listening ear more than anything else).

Answer the above question (i.e., Why do I keep *choosing* unsafety?) **if, for example, you find yourself living in perpetual victimhood while constantly blaming someone else** (e.g., your husband, your parents, your culture, your religion, etc.) **while you *also* no longer want to live with this perpetual anger, resentment, or misery.**

NOTE: If you begin to feel too emotionally overwhelmed as you answer this question, stop and step away from it for a while. Then come back when you feel ready. If you find that you are consistently emotionally overwhelmed or upset each time you try to answer this question, it is most likely time to seek help from a trauma-informed mental health professional, so that you can begin healing your underlying emotional dysregulation.

In any case, if you do decide to answer this question, **I invite you to do so in a gentle space of self-honesty and compassionate accountability,** as I discuss in the following two closing chapters of Part Two, the latter of which includes my own answer to this difficult question.

68

Surrender to Uncomfortable Self-Honesty and Compassionate Accountability

I know that the last RE-CAP question ("Why do I keep *choosing* unsafety?") might be emotionally painful, especially if you are still trapped in performing femininity or if you are still holding onto the belief that being a "good woman" is about showing up in helpless passivity and remaining committed to patient suffering (a mindset that I myself was trapped in for many years).

However, if you do find that the question resonates, even if painfully so, I think you'll find that getting honest with yourself right now is much less painful than being *forced* to get honest with yourself later on (which is, unfortunately, what happened to me). This is because if we live long enough, at some point, nearly all of us (male and female) will face a personal trial or a series of personal trials that are so difficult, so humiliating, or so painfully soul-crushing that we have no other choice but to face the reality of ourselves. In this moment, it can feel as if we are watching a scary movie in life-sized "technicolor" while *we* are the main character recklessly ruining their life.

I myself remember feeling like I was on the movie set of my own life and then finding that I was *voluntarily* playing the central role of the "helpless woman" ruining her life. And by "voluntarily," I mean I was not being paid or compensated for all my sacrificial work in the role of feminine helplessness (though I would pay for it mightily).

As I began to wake up from this trance of pious passivity, I strongly disliked the life-sized reflection of "me" staring back at me. Nevertheless, the painful trials that had brought me to this place were enough to convince me that it was in my best interest to neither turn away from what I saw nor cast blame on someone else.

In this glaringly accurate, painful reflection of my *real* life story—wherein I didn't allow myself to claim the victim role as central to my life (even as I fully acknowledged where I was in fact the victim of calculated harm)—I was forced to face the shadows of my *nafs* and the darknesses of my own soul.

I then went a step further and owned up to the choices that *I myself made* that had brought me to that particular juncture of my life—even if I didn't make those harmful choices intentionally.

Toward Compassionate Accountability

So, dear reader, if you *can* sit patiently in the incredible discomfort of asking yourself the question, "Why am I *choosing* unsafety?" (even if not today, but whenever you're ready), I think you'll find a whole new world of self-healing, soul-nourishing joy, and personal transformation waiting for you on the other side. That is, if you answer it both honestly *and* compassionately, and without falling into toxic self-blame or victimhood (e.g., without feeling like you're a horrible person and without perceiving the question as "blaming the victim").

Your honesty allows you to see where you could have made different choices in life, and your compassion allows you to see where your past circumstances made those different choices nearly impossible. Additionally, your compassion allows you to see where your current circumstances are making those different choices very challenging, painful, or risky for you. Nevertheless, you commit to at least one small step toward self-betterment each day.

This approach to self-healing, self-honesty, and personal transformation is what I call compassionate accountability.

Answering the Question Myself

During my own journey of self-healing, self-honesty, and personal transformation, I have had to sit with this question more than once. Some days I still sit with it today—as I share in the following chapter entitled, "But Why Am I Choosing Unsafety?"

Till today, this single question remains one of the most difficult and transformative questions that I have ever challenged myself to honestly answer. This is because while answering it, I didn't allow myself to deflect blame or to shift focus onto someone else, even when there were in fact others who had deliberately caused me harm. Instead, I challenged myself to sit in a place of unfiltered, painful honesty—emotionally, intimately, and spiritually—while also challenging myself to be self-compassionate and non-judgmental of whatever came up.

Then I challenged myself to *gently* hold myself accountable for being better to myself and making better choices for my life and soul—consistently. It wasn't always easy. In fact, it has *never* been easy. But I have found that after taking small manageable steps each day, it has gotten easier.

Yet still, there are moments that I find myself unconsciously slipping back into the cozy familiarity of victimhood and female helplessness—because this is what I mistook for pious femininity for so many years of my life. In my moments of self-awareness in this emotional spiral, I lean most into self-compassion and self-forgiveness, until I feel safe enough to hold myself accountable again.

69

But Why Am I Choosing Unsafety?

"We began asking ourselves… Why are close relationships, which are supposed to be about love, often so painful? What are we doing that causes the pain? What are we overlooking? How can we have more love and less pain? The answers came, not always in the way we expected or in a kindly manner. Sometimes we were so stubborn and resistant to learning that life had to take a sledgehammer approach to teaching us."
—Gay and Kathleen Hendricks, PhDs, *Conscious Loving: The Journey to Co-Commitment*

One of the most painful and memorable "sledgehammer" lessons that shocked me out of the debilitating victimhood of performing femininity and into the rejuvenating accountability of embodying femininity was right before I walked away from my second marriage for the last time. A series of emotionally damaging events forced me to face this fact about the relationship that I had chosen for myself: My "Islamic marriage" wasn't the divinely gifted soul-mate connection that I had initially processed it as (and claimed it to be). Instead, it was a divinely decreed co-dependent, trauma-bond that I had (albeit unconsciously) brought upon myself.

Today, I am grateful for this painful experience, which I call a blessing and a challenge. This is because it was the mutually created nature of this toxic relationship that my

Merciful, All-Wise Creator used to wake me up to the fact that I was in a toxic relationship with myself.

And I had been for quite some time.

Unsafety Felt Familiar to Me

If I were to summarize into a single sentence why I kept choosing unsafety in the name of love and companionship, it would be this: *I keep choosing unsafety because unsafety feels most familiar to me.* No, I wasn't choosing this painful familiarity consciously or intentionally. But the fact still stands that I was *choosing* it, nonetheless.

Remember how earlier in this book, I mentioned three unintended side effects of my "tough love" upbringing? They were:

1) I went through my childhood and young adulthood feeling that nothing I felt or thought mattered.
2) I went through childhood and young adulthood feeling that *I* didn't matter.
3) I went through childhood and young adulthood feeling that nowhere was safe to authentically exist in this world, not even my own home.

Today, as I link past experiences to present challenges, I find it unsettling to realize that I could simply replace the words *childhood and young adulthood* with "marriage and religious practice" and the painful truth of these statements would remain. So, this much is also true:

1) I went through my marriage and religious practice feeling like nothing I felt or thought mattered.
2) I went through marriage and religious practice feeling that *I* didn't matter.
3) I went through marriage and religious practice feeling that nowhere was safe to authentically exist in this world, not even my own home—or in my own soul.

So, for me, unsafety and emotional suffering didn't just feel *familiar*. It felt *pious*. And it also felt like home.

How I Reset My Life and Soul

If I were to summarize into a single sentence what I did to turn my personal and spiritual life around, it would be this: *I chose soul-nourishing growth over toxic stability and co-dependency, and I chose compassionate accountability over toxic self-blame and helpless victimhood.*

In other words, I committed to my own Feminine Soul Reset. No, this journey hasn't been easy—far from it. In many ways, it remains deeply challenging till today. In fact, here is one of the promises I made to myself on this journey that I've found the most difficult to keep: **I'm willing to sacrifice my reputation in front of people, but I'm not willing to sacrifice my soul in front of Allah.**

Today, I continue to strive upon this level of self-honesty and self-love, and I continuously beg Allah's assistance.

As the saying goes: *This isn't for the fainthearted.* And by "this" I mean the journeys of soul-nourishing self-love and of transitioning from performing femininity to embodying femininity.

Yet still, the rewards I've received—and continue to receive—from this commitment to self-honesty, personal authenticity, and spiritual wellness (even when I fall short at times) are ones that I wouldn't trade for the world.

PART THREE
Let's Heal Together and Love Together: Five Ways Forward

"Show up with joy and overflowing love, always. When you share these joyful, loving moments with another person, you're not investing in a future with them so much as you're investing in a future with yourself. So, pour all your love and joy into this moment that you're sharing in the 'now.' Because the now is all you have, especially with the ones you love. As far as future investments go, how you show up in this present moment is more than anything an investment in the relationship you'll have with yourself for the rest of your life. In this way, you love freely—without fetters on yourself and without chains on your heart. And this gives you and your soul companion the best possibility of everlasting love. But even if you're not granted that rare divine gift with someone else, you'll at least enjoy everlasting love 'forever now'—with yourself."
—from the journal of Umm Zakiyyah

70

Who Will Catch Her When She Falls?

Remember those trust games they'd have us do at camps and retreats? I'm talking about the ones where you face forward and then calmly fall backwards into the safety of someone's arms who is standing behind you and below you. Or you calmly fall backwards into a group of arms banded firmly together to catch you, protect you, and keep you safe when you fall.

Most of us have probably participated in this trust exercise at least once in our lives. If not, then we've likely at least watched our friends and classmates participate. So, keeping this trust game in mind, I want you to imagine this:

An argument breaks out between the ones assigned to fall backwards and the ones assigned to catch them. This argument becomes increasingly bitter until each group is saying the most hurtful things to the other group. Then when the time of the trust game arrives, here's what happens: The ones assigned to fall backwards don't feel comfortable trusting the ones assigned to catch them, and the ones assigned to catch them don't feel inspired to just stand there creating a safety net for people who don't appreciate them or who think so badly about them.

So, in anger and frustration, both groups say, "Let's just stop these stupid trust games altogether!"

But the truth is, deep down, each and every person in *both* groups, really wants to go back to doing the trust games. Not only because they were so much fun, but also because they brought everyone's hearts together like no other game could.

When a few of them get to talking, they discover that neither side really wanted to stop the games; they just wanted to stop feeling all that anger, bitterness, and pain that was triggered with all the bickering and insults. So, now the mere sight of the other group is a constant reminder of all the hurtful things the other group *really* feels about them.

But after some tense back and forth, both groups reluctantly agree to give the game another try.

Loss of Trust on the Altar of Blame

Just as the trust game is about to be rekindled, another problem arises: Neither group wants to be the first to fulfill their assigned role.

The ones assigned to fall backwards start saying, "I'm not going up there until I know for sure they're going to catch me!" Then the ones assigned to catch them start saying, "I'm not going to stand there locking arms for nothing! If you won't go up there and trust that I'll catch you, then I'm not standing there at all!"

Then some assigned mediators come in and try to convince both sides to just fulfill their role, while avoiding focusing on what the other group is supposed to be doing. "One of you has to trust first," they say. "Who will it be?"

71

Who Will Step Up First?

Now, you're probably wondering, "What's the point of this trust-game story?"

Well, the point is this: I'm sharing this "trust game" story as an analogy to the infamous "gender war" that is happening today between men and women, wherein trust is being increasingly (and bitterly) lost between us. So, I ask, "Who will be the first to fulfill their assigned role—regardless of what the other group is or is not doing to fulfill theirs?"

Here, I'm asking this in the wider community context more than in the private family context (though it certainly applies privately in our homes as well).

But before you answer, I ask you to reflect deeply on four additional questions—still using the trust game analogy—as they relate to how we should move forward as a community:

1) Who *should* be the first to stand up and fulfill their role and simply do what they were assigned to do?

2) Whose role fulfillment is most likely to inspire the other to naturally follow in fulfilling theirs?

3) If the ones assigned as the "safety net" fulfill their role first, what are they risking if, worst case scenario, the ones assigned to fall into their arms never fulfill theirs?

4) If the ones assigned to fall backwards fulfill their role first, what are they risking if, worst case scenario, the

ones assigned to catch them aren't there when they fall?

It's Not About Who's to Blame

As you reflect honestly and deeply on each question, keep this in mind: I'm not asking who carries more of the *blame* for the loss of trust we're facing. I'm not asking who's more at fault for what the other is going through. And I'm not suggesting that any group is absolved of fulfilling their assigned role (or at least of sincerely preparing to fulfill it).

In the end, I'm asking one question and one question only: *Who carries the greater degree of responsibility in leading us out of this relationship crisis we've found ourselves in?*

I'll give you a hint.

In the Qur'an, Allah says:

وَلَهُنَّ مِثْلُ ٱلَّذِى عَلَيْهِنَّ بِٱلْمَعْرُوفِ ۚ وَلِلرِّجَالِ عَلَيْهِنَّ دَرَجَةٌ ۗ وَٱللَّهُ عَزِيزٌ حَكِيمٌ ﴿٢٢٨﴾

"...And they (women) have rights similar (to those of their husbands) over them according to what is reasonable. But men have a degree [of responsibility] over them. And Allah is Exalted in Might [and] Wise."
—*Al-Baqarah* (2:228)

In any case, no matter who decides to trust first, we as men and women can still heal together, and we can love together—if we really want to. **Here are five (5) ways forward for men and women:**

FIVE STEPS
Toward Mutual Love and Intimacy

"*When any problem occurs, you have two choices: you can get upset about it, or you can simply figure out what needs to be done. Getting upset has a seductive quality to it; there is rich drama to be had there. The cost is that there is no happiness to be had. Happiness opens up when you drop the drama and start looking for what needs to be done. Any relationship improves when both people shift from complaints to statements of what they want.*"
—Gay and Kathleen Hendricks, PhDs, *Conscious Loving: The Journey to Co-Commitment*

"*Remember, we aren't controlling others with our goals—we are trying to give direction to* our *life.*"
—Melody Beattie, *The Language of Letting Go: Daily Meditations on Codependency*

72

Take Responsibility for Your Own Life and Soul

Step 1 for Men
Take responsibility for your own life and soul. How?

Look deep within and sincerely ask yourself what you want from life, personally and spiritually. Then seek to attain it without outsourcing your manhood or sense of self. No external achievement or relationship can define who you are or determine your worth.

A relationship isn't a place where you prove your manhood or where you seek to control someone else or play savior. It's a place to grow into the best version of yourself while providing safety and protection to those under your care.

Step 1 for Women
Take responsibility for your own life and soul. How?

Look deep within and sincerely ask yourself what you want from life, personally and spiritually. Then seek to attain it without abandoning yourself, without lowering your standards, and without disappearing yourself from existence in hopes of being loved and seen.

No human being can save you, rescue from yourself, or love you more than you're willing to love yourself.

A relationship isn't a place where you find love and happiness. It's a place where you share love and happiness.

73

Prioritize Your Relationship with Your Creator and Yourself

Step 2 for Men
Prioritize your relationship with your Creator and yourself.

Develop such a deep relationship with your Creator that you don't consciously or unconsciously ask (or demand) that a woman shows up for you in ways you haven't shown up for yourself. So, whether it's continuous sacrifice for your own self-betterment or words and affirmations for your own personal elevation as a man, or it's desiring a life of ease without financial distress, seek this from Allah alone and from within yourself.

Do this with a mindset of abundance rooted in taqwaa, wherein nothing your loved ones need or want from you threaten your holistic wealth. In doing so, reflect on the prophetic hadith:

الْغِنَى فِي الْقَلْبِ وَالْفَقْرُ فِي الْقَلْبِ مَنْ كَانَ الْغِنَى فِي قَلْبِهِ لا يَضُرُّهُ مَا لَقِيَ مِنَ الدُّنْيَا وَمَنْ كَانَ الْفَقْرُ فِي قَلْبِهِ فَلا يُغْنِيهِ مَا أَكْثَرَ لَهُ فِي الدُّنْيَا وَإِنَّمَا يَضُرُّ نَفْسَهُ شُحُّها

"Wealth is in the heart and poverty is in the heart. Whoever is wealthy in his heart will not be harmed no matter what happens in the world. Whoever is impoverished in his heart will not be satisfied no matter how much he has in the world. Verily, he will only be harmed by the greed of his own soul" (*al-Mu'jam al-Kabīr* 1643, Grade: *Sahih*).

Step 2 for Women
Prioritize your relationship with your Creator and yourself.

Develop such a deep relationship with your Creator that you don't consciously or unconsciously seek from a man what only Allah can provide. So, whether it is unwavering protection, abundant provision, or lasting happiness, seek it from Allah alone.

Then look within to discover how you can gift it to yourself with His help. And then love and support your husband from this secure place of self-love rooted in taqwaa (piety and protecting your own soul from harm). In doing so, reflect deeply on the prophetic hadith shared above. Also, this quote from Dr. LePara's book is one I find helpful:

"She read about how to heal self-betrayal by rebuilding the trust you have with yourself, and was inspired to take a meaningful step forward. She decided to make and keep one small daily promise to support her health—the smaller and more sustainable, the better."
—Dr. Nicole LePara, *How to Do the Work: Recognize Your Patterns, Heal from Your Past, and Create Your Self*

74

Get Curious Alone and Together

Step 3 for Men and Women
Get curious alone and together.

Before entering a relationship or before ending a relationship (and for men: before choosing polygyny), get curious about how your unmet needs in childhood are showing up in your life today. Get curious about how these past wounds are influencing how you are showing up in your relationships, especially the one you have with yourself.

Then get curious about how you can be compassionate and supportive to yourself and then to your partner as you both heal your individual wounds and begin to meet your own needs.

"If we weren't trying to control whether a person liked us or his or her reaction to us, what would we do differently? If we weren't trying to control the course of a relationship, what would we do differently? If we weren't trying to control another person's behavior, how would we think, feel, speak, and behave differently than we do now?
...Make a list, then do it."
—Melody Beattie, *The Language of Letting Go*

75

Give Each Other Space to Enjoy Life

Step 4 for Men and Women
Give each other space to enjoy life individually and together.

No healthy relationship can thrive without boundaries and joy. This joy must come from what you do in your own space and circles, as well as what you do in your shared space as a couple and as a family.

Boundaries are the lines you draw to protect your mental, emotional, and spiritual health. We all need them, so respect them in yourself and in your partner, even if you don't understand them. But be sure to discuss them first to avoid confusion. This is how you preserve and nurture joy.

"Co-Commitment 6: I commit myself to having a good time in my close relationships. It may seem odd that we would need to make a formal commitment to enjoyment…Committing yourself to enjoyment in your relationships can be one of the most liberating moves you can make, because it opens the possibility of conflict-free relationships."
—Gay and Kathleen Hendricks, PhDs, *Conscious Loving: The Journey to Co-Commitment*

76

Forgive and Overlook As a Lifestyle

Step 5 for Men and Women
Forgive and overlook wherever possible and reasonable.

You know when forgiveness and compassion become most difficult? When you put unrealistic expectations on other people and when you project onto others standards of love and commitment that you're unwilling to give to yourself.

So, if your first thoughts of a "happy marriage" evoke images of what you'll be getting *from* someone or what they'll be doing *for* you, then take a step back. Then ask yourself: Why am I not *most* excited about pouring my own deeply felt love and joy into my soul companion and our relationship? Then renew your commitment to yourself and each other, but now in a space of forgiveness, compassion, and taqwaa.

"If you want to begin a journey of forgiveness in your marriage, it's best to start within yourself. When we struggle mightily with forgiving a loved one, it's often because we haven't sat compassionately with the darknesses within ourselves. Only when you sit with your own darknesses can you genuinely hold space for theirs."
—from the journal of Umm Zakiyyah

Epilogue

*Believe in Unseen Possibilities of Love
and Intimacy*

A Gentle Reminder to Believing Souls

The first description of the people of taqwaa in the Qur'an
is that they believe in the *ghayb,* which encompasses all the
unseen realities and possibilities beyond human perception,
imagination, or experience.

So, don't limit what you believe is possible for yourself
and your relationship based on fear, past experience,
emotional wounding, or even what problems are visibly and
truthfully in front of you.

With sincere taqwaa, there is *nothing* that is impossible for
you and your soul companion—or for this ummah of
believing men and women—whether individually or
together, with the help of Allah.

———————————————————

*May Allah forgive our sins, cover our faults, and help us guard our
tongues. May He purify our hearts and remove from us any ill feeling
or animosity toward each other.*
*May He place in our hearts compassion, empathy, and love for His
sake. May He remove from us any speech or actions that divide the
hearts of the believers. And may He grant us excellent character such*

that we are a mercy to all who meet us, as His beloved Prophet and Messenger (peace be upon him) was a mercy to all of mankind.

Read an excerpt from

Before You Become His Garment in Marriage:
Do's and Don'ts for Muslim Women
by Umm Zakiyyah

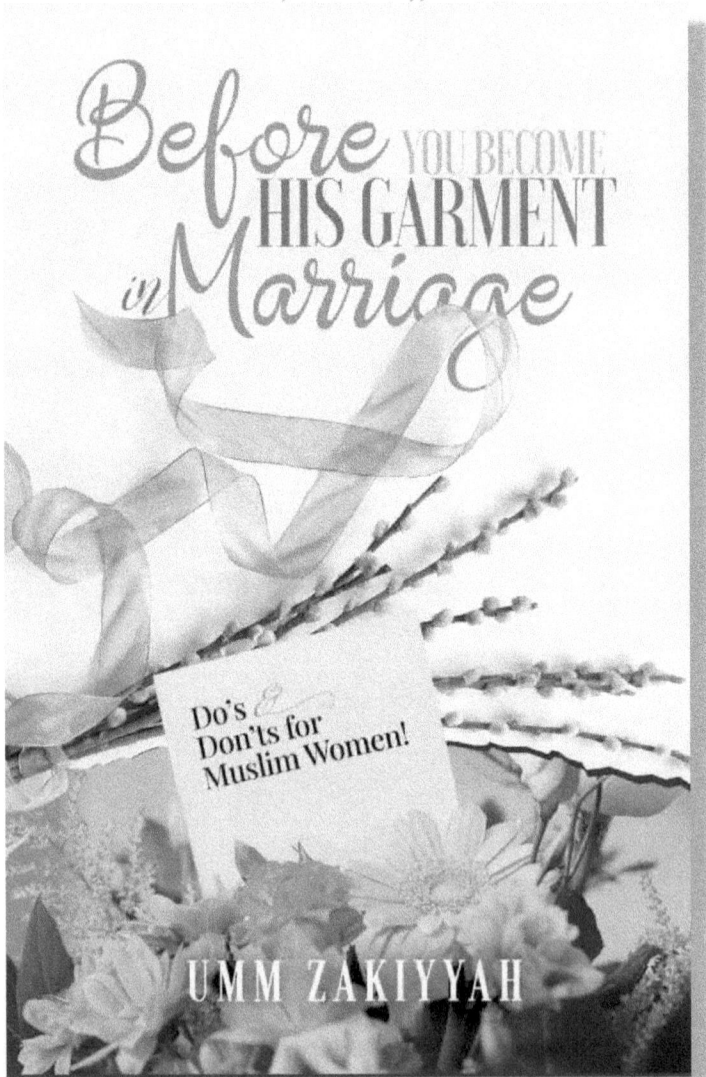

I remember when I first began getting official marriage proposals. I was around seventeen years old. I had a long list of questions I would ask anyone who came to ask about me.

Years later my daughter's father would tell me he felt like he was taking a test and solving "brain teaser" puzzles. He'd say it jokingly, and we'd both get a good laugh out of it.

At the time, I had written down as many questions as I could think of, and for me at the time, that represented my level best of showing up authentically as myself.

Once I selected my soul companion for marriage, I was mentally prepared to do everything I could to serve and please him and avoid even the chance of divorce. As a youth, I genuinely imagined that this was everything I needed to go into a marriage fully prepared and to protect my marriage from ever dying.

However, over the years, life has taught me that, as undesirable as divorce is, there are things worse than a dying marriage—the worst of which is a dying soul. I learned that you could stay married and lose yourself. I learned that you could never even consider divorce but lose your faith. I learned that you could look happy on the outside and be suffering emotional pain on the inside. I learned that you could preserve your relationships with your husband and loved ones while sacrificing your relationship with Allah.

When I booked my official first RTT session as a client, I wanted to find out why I so often woke up feeling emotionally exhausted, mentally spent, and overcome with weighty dread about facing the day ahead. I also wanted to understand why it was so challenging for me to show up for myself with joy, mental calm, and self-love.

I had already done a psychotherapy session with another therapy practitioner and had been part of numerous support groups over the years. But still, I kept hitting these roadblocks: I struggled to actually enjoy my daily self-care routines, I found it difficult to feel comfortable and at ease while expanding my business, and I continuously felt disinclined to move forward with so many of the things I loved and wanted in my life.

During the RTT session, my therapist asked me to take in a deep breath and relax (as is standard in a Rapid Transformational Therapy session) so that I could quiet the chatter of my conscious mind and calmly recall what was at the root of these roadblocks. In this, she was guiding me to relax my overall nervous system and thus activate a parasympathetic response. This relaxation technique allowed me to access the pictures and words stored in the "safety toolbox" of my mind that discouraged me from showing up to my life with joy, mental calm, and self-love.

In one scene (which is what we call a mental memory in RTT) I saw myself at around fourteen years old sitting in the passenger seat of a car next to a male relative (whom I'll call Walad) who was about ten years my elder and had come to the city to visit our family.

In this scene, I saw Walad become suddenly angry with me then threaten to forcibly remove me from his car and abandon me on the side of the road. In the mental memory, I recalled learning that this threat of violence had erupted due to me expressing a different perspective from him during a casual conversation we'd been having as he drove me home.

After this scene replayed in my mind, I was asked to link this incident (and two other earlier mental memories) to my current mental roadblocks. In other words, my therapist was asking me to connect this memory of Walad to the reason that it was so difficult for me to embrace joy, mental peace, and self-love and to pursue the life I wanted while fully embracing the things I loved.

As my RTT practitioner and I discussed the links between these early mental memories and how I showed up in my life today, I was surprised that there had been any significant link at all between Walad's treatment of me when I was a teenager and how I showed up for myself as a grown woman.

Consciously, after repeated negative and threatening experiences with Walad, I had told myself years ago that I would simply keep ties with him and treat him kindly, but otherwise I'd keep my distance since he was so mercurial, unsafe, and potentially violent.

As my therapist and I continued exploring what had actually come up while my nervous system was in a relaxed state, I realized that this "moving picture" in my mind from fourteen years old (along with a couple of others) had implanted the following "feeling words" in my nafs and were then mentally stored in the "safety toolbox" of my mind:

As a female soul in this world, it's not safe for you to feel relaxed and carefree because this could expose you to danger or abandonment. As a female, your job is to shrink yourself to make sure that the men in your life feel good about themselves and are not offended or angered by your thoughts and feelings. So, as a woman, it's not safe for you to pursue the things you want and love. Besides, as a "good Muslim woman," you'll one day have to give up everything that makes you happy if the man in your life wants you to, even if you're doing nothing wrong or displeasing to your Creator.

That's when I had another epiphany. Nearly every single man I had allowed into my intimate space emotionally, with rare exceptions, held some version of one or more of these beliefs about women in relation to himself:

You don't have the right to think, feel, or express anything I don't like. It is your job to patiently stand by my side while I freely live my life and do whatever I want, even if it hurts you deeply. If you're really a good woman, you would give up everything you want to make me happy. It is your job to keep quiet and learn from me because none of your knowledge or experience matters if it doesn't align with mine. I value your intelligence and talents only insomuch as they make me feel good about myself for "conquering" or "owning" someone like you.

Then I recalled that I had experienced over and over some version of the initial Walad incident in so many of my interactions with men later in life. Realizing this inspired a deeper epiphany for me: The picture that I had in my mind of what a "man" looked like was various versions of Walad: threatening, entitled, and insecure.

So, unconsciously, I'd felt that the most that I could hope for in a good man was that he wasn't threatening. Anything else (i.e., entitlement and insecurity), I'd unconsciously assumed, came along with having any man at all.

That was why when I looked for a "good man," I'd continuously sought or accepted someone who "wouldn't mind" if I pursued the things I loved and wanted in life. What this meant in practical reality was securing for myself a "man in flesh" who was a manifestation of the unconscious plea of the shrinking little girl inside me: *I know it disturbs you deeply that I have a life outside of you, but please just don't harm me emotionally, verbally, or physically whenever I do the things I love. That's all I ask.*

It was both chilling and profound to discover that I had been living all my adult life—even as a forty something divorced woman now on my own—shrinking and apologizing to men for my existence as an intelligent, vibrant female soul in this world. That was when I realized it was time for me to reembrace my worth and honor my needs…

READ MORE

at
uzauthor.com *or* **uzhearthub.com**

Glossary of Select Arabic and Islamic Terms

Allah: Arabic term for God; the only One who has the right to be worshipped

'ajalah: haste, unrest, restlessness

anaah: calm forbearance; equanimity; mindfulness

ayaat: plural form of *ayah*

ayah: verse from Qur'an or divine sign

bi'idhnillaah: "with the help of Allah (the Creator)"

da'wah: teaching others about Islam; inviting others to spiritual guidance

deen: spiritual way of life; religion

emaan: sincere faith; authentic spirituality; belief in Islam

fiqh: Islamic law or jurisprudence

fitnah: difficult trial

fitrah: inherent inborn nature of every human soul to surrender themselves in worship to their Creator alone, and to live authentically in a spiritually and morally upright life

ghayb: unseen world and reality known only to Allah

hadith: prophetic narration

halaal: permissible and divinely blessed

hayaa': shyness or healthy sense of shame

husnu dhann: assuming the best about someone or something or assigning the best possible meaning or intention to someone or something

inshaa'Allah: God-willing

Istikhaarah: prayer and supplication for making a decision about something

Jahiliyyah: pre-Islamic days of spiritual and moral ignorance before the prophetic assignment was given to Prophet Muhammad (peace be upon him); any mindset or life path that mirrors this spiritual and moral ignorance

khushoo': sincerity and humility of the heart and soul; deep concentration in *Salaah* such that the heart is consistently spiritually nourished by its sincere and humble connection to its Creator in every part of prayer

mahr: obligatory gift given to woman upon marriage; dowry

nafs: human inner self made up of the complex interconnectedness of a person's soul, mind, heart, and body; sometimes refers to a person's desires that are self-serving and spiritually harmful

qadar: divine decree; predestination

qawwaam/qawwaamah: the man's divinely assigned role of being the maintainer, provider, and protector of women and of female safety and wellness in the home and society

Rabb: another name for Allah that refers to His Lordship over creation; Creator, Owner and Manager of all that exists

sadaqah: voluntary, non-obligatory charity

Shaytaan: the devil; Satan

shirk: assigning divine attributes to creation or creation's attributes to the Creator; paganism

shukr: sincere gratefulness, thankfulness or gratitude

soo'u dhann: assuming the worst about someone or something or assigning the worst possible meaning or intention to someone or something

Sunnah: prophetic guidance or example; the life and teachings of Prophet Muhammad (peace and blessings be upon him)

sujood: another term for *sajdah:* prostrating the forehead on the floor in submission to Allah

Surah: divine chapter of the Qur'an

taqwaa: sincere God-consciousness and daily soul care that protects the heart from corruption and the soul from spiritual harm in the Hereafter

tawakkul: sincere trust in the wisdom and decisions of the Creator

REFERENCES

Angum F, Khan T, Kaler J, Siddiqui L, Hussain A. The Prevalence of Autoimmune Disorders in Women: A Narrative Review. *Cureus.* 2020 May 13;12(5):e8094. doi: 10.7759/cureus.8094, cited in Pugle, M. "Why Autoimmune Diseases Affect More Women Than Men." Retrieved March 5, 2024 from: https://www.verywellhealth.com/why-autoimmune-diseases-affect-more-women-5095040

Bandura, A. (1990) "Selective Activation and Disengagement of Moral Control." *Journal of Social Issues* vol 46 no. 1 pg 27-46. January 1, 1990.

Beezle_33228 (2023). "I've recently realized that I've been masking my entire life, and now I don't know who I am." Reddit.com. Retrieved February 1, 2025 from: https://www.reddit.com/r/AutismInWomen/comments/104a8u7/ive_recently_realized_that_ive_been_masking_my/

Bradshaw, J. (2005). *Healing the Shame that Binds You.* Health Communications Inc. October 15, 2005.

Chan, K. (2024). "So, Should I Be Dating a Beta Male? They're sweet, kind, loyal...the list goes on" VeryWellMind.com (June 13, 2024). Retrieved December 14, 2024 from: https://www.verywellmind.com/beta-male-8658879

Cressman, D. (2022). "I Feel Like I Have to Change Who I Am to Have a Man in My Life." The Good Men Project. February 3, 2022 Retrieved March 26, 2024 from: https://goodmenproject.com/featured-content/i-feel-like-i-have-to-change-who-i-am-to-have-a-man-in-my-life/

Differences of opinion between husband and wife concerning matters where the scholars differed. IslamQA.com. Retrieved August 27, 2023 from: https://islamqa.info/en/answers/97125/differences-of-opinion-between-husband-and-wife-concerning-matters-where-the-scholars-differed

Elshinawy, M. (2021). "Ḥayāʾ: More Than Just Modesty in Islam." Yaqeen Institute. August 5, 2021. Retrieved December 23, 2024 from: https://yaqeeninstitute.org/read/paper/haya-more-than-just-modesty

Goleman, D. (2006). *Social Intelligence: The New Science of Human Relationship*s. Random House LLC. New York, USA.

Gottman, J. et al. (2016). *The Man's Guide to Women: Scientifically Proven Secrets from the Love Lab About What Women Really Want.* Rodale Books. February 2, 2016.

Kovanen, M. (2004). "8 Consequences of the Father Wound on Well-Being and Relationships." Alive Counselling. Retrieved December 8, 2024 from: https://alivecounselling.com/counselling-resources/how-our-family-relationships-impacts-us-the-father-wound/

LePara, N. (2021). *How to Do the Work: Recognize Your Patterns, Heal from Your Past, and Create Your Self.* Harper. March 9, 2021

Letzer, R. (2016). "There's no such thing as an alpha male" *Business Insider.* October 12, 1016. Retrieved January 9, 2025 from: https://www.businessinsider.com/no-such-thing-alpha-male-2016-10

"Masking in mental health conditions." (2022) SmartTMS: Mending Minds. Retrieved February 1, 2025 from: https://www.smarttms.co.uk/masking-in-mental-health-conditions/

Maté, G. (2023) "How Being Too Nice Can Destroy You: A Story You've Never Heard." (September 10, 2023) via Your Inner Child Matters YouTube channel. https://www.youtube.com/watch?v=xChNbQ2o0Ro

"'Nice people' more likely to get autoimmune diseases; women even more." (Aug 23, 2023) TimesofIndia.com. Retrieved March 5, 2024 from:
https://timesofindia.indiatimes.com/life-style/health-fitness/health-news/nice-people-more-likely-to-get-autoimmune-diseases-women-even-more/photostory/102909238.cms

One_Control5185 (2023). "Is anyone else incredibly judgmental and critical of others?" Reddit.com. Retrieved February 7, 2025 from:
https://www.reddit.com/r/CPTSD/comments/155azc1/is_anyone_else_incredibly_judgmental_and_critical/

Pappas, S. and Bryner J. (2023). "Is the Alpha Wolf Idea a Myth?" *Scientific American*. February 28, 2023. Retrieved January, 9, 2025 from:
https://www.scientificamerican.com/article/is-the-alpha-wolf-idea-a-myth/

"Speaking of Health: Tips for embracing joy in daily life," Mayo Clinic Health System. Retrieved August 26, 2024 from:
https://www.mayoclinichealthsystem.org/hometown-health/speaking-of-health/tips-for-embracing-joy-in-daily-life

Steinberg. M (2024). "Emotional Addiction." MarkSteinberg.com. Retrieved December 9, 2024 from:
https://marksteinberg.com/webpages/writings/emotional-addiction.jsp

Vault Empowers (2025) "Men don't marry who they want to marry because they're not healed" with Jason Wilson. Interview by Brandi Harvey (February 5, 2025) via Vault Empowers YouTube channel.
https://www.youtube.com/watch?v=M0ZubyffrA0&t=97s

About the Author

Known for her soul-touching books and spiritual reflections on emotional healing, Umm Zakiyyah is a world-renowned author, speaker, and soul-care mentor. She specializes in supporting women of faith transform into the best version of themselves—personally, emotionally, and spiritually.

Also known by her birth name Ruby Moore and her "Muslim name" Baiyinah Siddeeq, Umm Zakiyyah is the internationally acclaimed, award-winning author of more than fifty books, including novels, short story collections, and self-help. Her books are used in high schools and universities in the United States and worldwide, and her work has been translated into multiple languages.

Her novel *His Other Wife* is now a short film (available on Prime Video).

Umm Zakiyyah is certified in Rapid Transformational Therapy ® (RTT) and hypnotherapy, qualifications she earned under the guidance of Marisa Peer, author of *I Am Enough*. She also holds a certificate in trauma and somatics.

Umm Zakiyyah studied Arabic, Qur'an, Islamic sciences, 'aqeedah, and tafseer in the USA, Egypt, and Saudi Arabia for more than fifteen years.

Umm Zakiyyah has a BA degree in Elementary Education, an MA in English Language Learning, and Cambridge's CELTA (Certificate in English Language Teaching to Adults).

She is currently based in Dallas, Texas (USA).

Connect with her online:
UZ books: uzauthor.com

Feminine Soul Reset: sqsoul.com
Our Beautiful Qur'an Journey: uzhearthub.com
Instagram/TikTok: @uzauthor
Email: uz@uzauthor.com